D0529431

APR   2003

AnimalWays

Bees

AnimalWays

Bees

MARTIN SCHWABACHER

BENCHMARK BOOKS

MARSHALL CAVENDISH
NEW YORK

For Melissa

With thanks to Dr. Dan Wharton, director of the Center Park Wildlife
Center, for his expert reading of this manuscript.

Special thanks to Dr. Michael S. Engel and John S. Ascher for their help
with the evolutionary timeline, and to all the friendly librarians at the
American Museum of Natural History.

Benchmark Books
Marshall Cavendish
99 White Plains Road
Tarrytown, NY 10591-9001
Website: www.marshallcavendish.com

Library of Congress Cataloging-in-Publication Data
Schwabacher, Martin.
Bees / by Martin Schwabacher.
p. cm. — (Animalways)
Summary: Describes the physical characteristics, behavior, habitat, and life cycle of
various types of bees.
Includes bibliographical references and index.
ISBN 0-7614-1392-8
1. Bees—Juvenile literature. [1. Bees.] I. Title. II. Series.
QL565.2 .S39   2002   595.79'9—dc21   2002000909

Photo Research by Candlepants Incorporated

Cover Photo: Corbis/Stephen Dalton

The photographs in this book are used by permission and through the courtesy of:
Photo Researchers, Saussez, Jacana, 2; Scott Camazine, 16, 18, 38, 47, 63, 68 (top), 74,
94; Stephen Dalton, 23, 56, 65, 79; Harry Rogers, 30 (bottom); Jerome Wexler: 42;
S. Camazine, K. Visscher, 48; Eric Grave, 52; Jany Sauvanet, 80; E. Hanumantha Rae, 81;
Ken Cavanaugh, 85; Richard Hutchings, 90 (bottom); M.T. Frazier/ PSU, 97; Rod Planck,
101; *Corbis*: Scott T. Smith, 9; Michael and Patricia Fogden, 30–31; Martin B. Withers, 31
(bottom); Anthony Bannister/Gallo Images, 41, 55; Treat Davidson/Frank Lane Picture
Agency, 45, 68 (bottom); Macduff Everton, 77; Robert Pickett, 93; Scott T. Smith, 98;
Gary W. Carter, back cover; *Art Resource, NY*: Image Select, 12; *Dr. Michael S. Engel*, 21,
22; *Animals Animals*, Donald Specker, 14; Patti Murray, 26; Ken G. Preston, 30 (top);
Victoria McCormick, 58; O.S.F., 60, 90 (top); Fritz Prenzel, 87; C. C. Lockwood, 88.

Printed in Italy

1 3 5 6 4 2

Contents

HERE ARE SOME OF THE MAIN PHYLA, CLASSES, AND ORDERS, WITH PHOTOGRAPHS OF A TYPICAL ANIMAL FROM EACH GROUP.

Animal Kingdom

CNIDARIANS

coral

ARTHROPODS
(animals with jointed limbs and external skeleton)

MOLLUSKS

squid

CRUSTACEANS

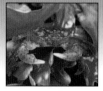

crab

ARACHNIDS

spider

INSECTS

BEE

MYRIAPODS

centipede

CARNIVORES

lion

SEA MAMMALS

whale

PRIMATES

orangutan

HERBIVORES
(5 orders)

elephant

ANNELIDS

earthworm

CHORDATES
(animals with a dorsal nerve chord)

ECHINODERMS

starfish

PHYLA

VERTEBRATES
(animals with a backbone)

SUB
PHYLA

FISH

fish

BIRDS

gull

MAMMALS

AMPHIBIANS

frog

REPTILES

snake

CLASSES

RODENTS

squirrel

INSECTIVORES

mole

MARSUPIALS

koala

SMALL MAMMALS
(several orders)

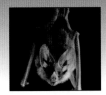

bat

ORDERS

1 The Amazing Bee

After flying several miles, a honeybee returns home to the hive, her stomach bulging. She is so full of nectar, the sweet liquid she gathered from hundreds of flowers, that her honey stomach now weighs more than the rest of her body.

The forager bee drops with a thud on the platform before the single door to her hive. Waiting to greet her are several guard bees, who look like palace bodyguards in a martial arts movie. They stand squarely on four hind legs, with two front legs raised in front of them, ready to fight. Before the guards let the arriving bee enter, they must make sure she is not a robber from another hive. They tap their antennae on the forager, checking for the distinctive smell of the hive, then let her pass.

On the way in, the forager passes another group of bees, the fanners. They crouch near the doorway, fanning their wings so fast that it is almost impossible to see them. The breeze sends cool air through the hive, keeping the thousands of workers

A HONEYBEE WADES THROUGH THE POLLEN-FILLED CENTER OF A FLOWER IN SEARCH OF FOOD.

inside comfortable. It is important that the hive not get too hot because it is filled with eggs, which must be kept at the correct temperature so the babies will hatch. Although all the worker bees are female, they almost never lay eggs. Every egg in the hive is laid by a single bee known as the queen, who is the mother of the colony's tens of thousands of workers, plus a few hundred males called drones.

Inside the hive, the returning forager shoulders past dozens of busy worker bees. Most ignore the new arrival, intent on their work. But several unloader bees are waiting near the door to accept deliveries. An unloader rushes up and taps her antennae on the forager bee's antennae, then unfolds her proboscis, forming a tube like an elephant's trunk. She sucks nectar from the forager's proboscis into her own honey stomach and hurries off.

The nectar is passed from bee to bee until thousands have a little. Many stand in the breeze with a drop of nectar in their jaws to dry and thicken it. This, along with chemicals from their bodies, begins turning the nectar into honey.

The honeybee hive is made of thousands of six-sided wax boxes, called cells. When a worker bee finds a cell that has been cleaned and polished for honey storage, it pumps the nectar into it. As the cell fills, workers gather around and fan it with their wings. The breeze causes the water to evaporate out of the nectar, leaving behind a thick, syrupy honey that is 87 percent sugar. With the water removed, bacteria and yeast cannot grow in the nectar and spoil it. When the cell is full of honey, builder bees seal it with a wax cup. The bees will eat the honey later—unless it is removed by humans or some other creature.

Every jar of honey in the world was made this way. Each drop starts out as nectar that is swallowed and carried inside a bee's stomach. It can take two thousand trips to gather enough nectar to make a single ounce of honey. Thousands of bees must visit thousands of flowers to make a single mouthful of the sweet, delicious honey we take for granted.

Nowadays, when sugary products surround us, our challenge is not so much to find sweets as to avoid eating too many. But until about four hundred years ago, the plants we now get sugar from did not even exist in Europe. People loved sweet things as much then as now—probably more, because they were rare—and honey satisfied that craving.

Bees also provided people with their first alcoholic drinks. Before ancient people learned to make beer, wine, or whiskey, they mixed honey with water and fermented it into a delicious alcoholic drink called mead. And before people had electric lights, beeswax was prized for making candles.

Today we have other sources of sugar, alcohol, and lighting, and honey and beeswax are not so important. But as more scientific research is done on bees, we have more and more reason to marvel at their complex societies. Most surprising of all was the discovery that bees have a language that is second only to human language in sophistication.

Though bees are still treasured for their sweet honey, they are now valued even more as essential partners in creating the other foods we eat. Only a tiny fraction of the 20,000 species of bees make honey. But all bees play a vital role in helping flowering plants create fruits, vegetables, and seeds.

Partners with Plants

Animals reproduce to replace themselves when they die. Plants must do the same thing. Their children are seeds, which grow into new plants.

In some ways, plant and animal reproduction is not that different. Just as animal babies are created by combining genes

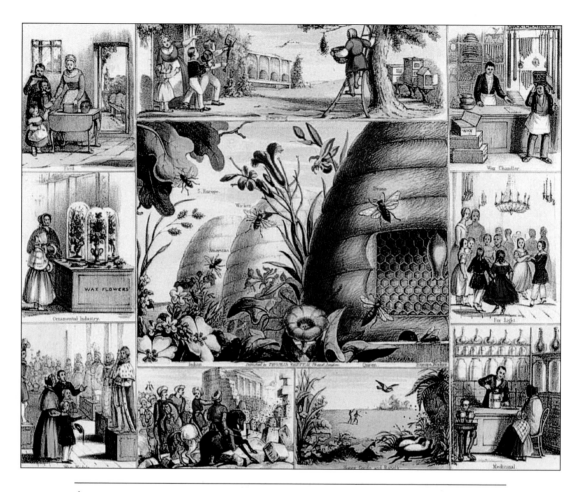

A HAND-COLORED LITHOGRAPH THAT WAS FIRST PUBLISHED IN LONDON AROUND 1850. IT SHOWS SCENES INVOLVING BEES AND HONEY.

from a father and a mother, seeds are created by combining genes from the male and female parts of plants—the flowers. The genetic material that is passed from the male to the female part of the plants is contained in a brightly colored powder called pollen.

The process of starting new seeds with pollen is called pollination. Some plants can pollinate themselves. Others must get pollen from another plant. For most flowering plants, this service is provided by bees.

As a bee crawls over a flower in search of nectar, it gets covered with pollen. The pollen falls on the bee's back or gets stuck in the hairs on its sides. When a bee moves from flower to flower, it leaves some pollen behind at each stop. Even though the bee brings most of the pollen back to the hive for food, the pollen grains that are left behind are enough to fertilize the plants. Bees can eat all they want and still pollinate plants because a bee can carry 50,000 pollen grains at one time. A few grains dropping off a bee at each flower is enough to keep a grove of apple trees fruitful and multiplying. A single apple blossom produces 70,000 grains of pollen, but it takes just ten grains to fertilize another flower. With no bees to pollinate the apple trees, however, the trees would produce just a few stunted apples. This reliance on bees is true for most other fruits and vegetables.

Bees, in turn, depend on flowers to survive. Pollen contains the exact mix of proteins and vitamins needed for bees' bodies to grow. Without the protein from pollen, bees could not lay eggs, and eggs could not grow into adult bees. The sugar in nectar provides the energy the bees need to work, fly, and make wax. Between nectar and pollen, bees get all the food they need from flowers.

It is no accident that flowers provide the perfect food for bees. Flowers and bees evolved together as partners. Those flowers that offered the food that bees liked the best were most likely to be visited by bees. Thus, such flowers were more likely to be pollinated. Over millions of years, these plants reproduced the most and became successful.

It is also no accident that bees are good pollinators. Plants that provided food to bees that were not good pollinators would not be pollinated. These plants died out, as did the bees that depended on them. Only bees that were good pollinators survived. By helping plants reproduce, they assured themselves of food the following year. The most successful bees were those that developed physical adaptations that aided pollen collection. That is

A HONEYBEE'S ENTIRE BODY IS DUSTED WITH POLLEN.

why all bees are covered with furry, branching hairs: the hairs help them to catch pollen.

Bees also developed behaviors that made them better pollinators. Many kinds of apple trees need pollen from another apple tree in order to be pollinated. If bees flew from an apple tree to an orange tree to a daisy, none of these plants would get the right pollen. Bee behavior evolved so that they always visit one kind of plant at a time when foraging. Bees are also better pollinators than butterflies, moths, and flies—which also like nectar—because these insects stop feeding when they are full. But bees keep foraging all day, collecting as much nectar as they can to make honey.

Because bees are the best pollinators, flowers that let only bees reach their nectar have come to dominate these flowers with more open-door policies. For instance, many flowers offer nectar only at the bottom of a narrow tube because bees have long tongues that can reach the bottom and many other insects do not.

Flowers Are for Bees

Pretty, sweet-smelling flowers do not exist to please people. All of the features that we prize about flowers arose to attract bees and other pollinators. To perform their task of pollinating flowers—and receive their reward of food—bees must first find the flowers. Plants with the biggest, brightest flowers attract the most bees because they are the easiest to see. In the competition to attract bees, flowers grew bigger and more brightly colored. Since bees locate flowers by scent as well as by sight, flowers also developed sweet smells.

Some plants do not need bees for pollination. They produce millions of pollen grains that blow away in the wind. Some of

POLLEN COMES IN A RAINBOW OF COLORS. YOU CAN TELL WHAT KIND OF FLOWERS A BEE HAS VISITED BY THE COLOR OF THE POLLEN ON ITS BODY.

the pollen lands on other flowers simply by chance. Most grasses and some trees reproduce this way. Wind-pollinated plants tend to have tiny, drab-colored, odorless blossoms because they do not need to attract bees.

Insect-pollinated flowers often have stripes on the petals pointing to the center. These stripes—like runways for airplanes—guide bees to the middle of the flower, where the nectar and pollen are. Bright spots in the center of the flower also serve as targets for flying bees. Some of these spots and stripes are invisible to humans, but visible to bees. This is because bees can see ultraviolet light, which the human eye cannot detect.

All bees are involved in this pollinating partnership, but not all bees can pollinate every plant. Some plants have a special relationship with certain kinds of bees. The nectar of red clover, for instance, cannot be reached by many races of honeybees, but certain bumblebees have longer tongues that can easily reach inside the red clover blossom. When people brought red clover to New Zealand, no insects living there could pollinate it. Only when bumblebees were brought to New Zealand could the red clover blossoms produce seeds. Around the world, many different species of bees have evolved just to pollinate the native plants.

Bees and Agriculture

Although honey and wax are both valuable products, bees' biggest contribution to agriculture is crop pollination.

People have known about insect pollination for about two hundred years. But only in the past century have we learned just how important bees are to plants' survival. As wild, bee-friendly land was cleared of weeds, there were no longer enough wild bees to pollinate farmers' crops. Without bees, plants produce much less fruit and vegetables, and what does grow is shrunken and odd-shaped. Farmers learned that when their orchards and fields are in bloom, it pays to hire a beekeeper to truck in several hundred bee colonies. The hives are placed in the center of the farm, and the bees are set loose to visit the millions of blossoms and pollinate them.

Honeybees are used the most because each colony contains thousands of bees and because their hives can be moved easily. But other bees are also used. Some alfalfa farmers provide

FLAVORS OF HONEY

Nectar is not all alike—each flower's nectar tastes slightly different. Because bees usually mix together the nectar from many flowers when making honey, these subtle flavors get lost. But when bees collect nectar from only one type of plant, the taste of the honey is distinctive. A tree's blossoms do not have the same flavor as its fruit, so orange-blossom honey does not taste like oranges. Lime-blossom honey has a crisp, minty taste with barely a hint of lime.

Beekeepers in England claim that honey from sweet clover (not common white clover) has a cinnamon flavor. Honey from wild clematis tastes like butter-scotch, and hawthorn has a nutty flavor. Honey made from herbs can be very flavorful. Rosemary honey has been popular in France for centuries, and honeys from sage, lavender, and marjoram are enjoyed in the Mediterranean region. A real treat is Tasmanian leatherwood honey, which comes from the forests of Australia. It is a delicious, spicy honey with a smell similar to that of sandalwood.

The oddest kind of honey does not come from nectar at all. Known as pine honey, it is made from honeydew, a sweet, sticky liquid left on evergreen trees by insects called aphids. When bees cannot find any nectar, they collect honeydew instead. It often turns black, moldy, and foul-tasting, but when it does not spoil, pine honey is considered a rare treat.

Most commercial honeys have been heated and filtered, which damages the flavor and nutrients. If you can find unheated, unfiltered honey—or honey still in the comb—you will taste the difference.

A HONEYBEE BURIES ITS HEAD IN A JEWELWEED BLOSSOM, SEARCHING FOR NECTAR.

permanent nest sites for two types of solitary bees, the alkali bee and the leafcutter bee. These bees don't produce honey, but they are perfect alfalfa pollinators and can make fields up to ten times more productive. Since there are thousands of kinds of bees, it is likely that more and more will be used in farming whenever a good match between bee and crop is found.

2 The Bee Family Tree

In 1986, several students from the University of Miami were hiking in Costa Rica. One student was exploring near a cave entrance when he suddenly started screaming. His friends looked up to see him surrounded by a dark cloud of bees. When the other students ran to help, the bees turned on them, too. The students were forced to flee, and two were stung so many times that they had to be hospitalized. After dark, when the bees had retreated, rescuers were finally able to reach the young man. But it was too late. He was dead. Caught between two rocks, he had been unable to run away and had been stung more than eight thousand times.

Most bees do not behave this way. They sting only to protect themselves. Some bees cannot sting at all. Over the years, as bee-keepers chose their favorite bees to breed, honeybees were bred to become more mild tempered. But human breeders can make mistakes. The bees that killed the young man in Costa Rica were the product of a breeding experiment gone wrong.

A 33-MILLION-YEAR-OLD FOSSIL OF AN EXTINCT HONEYBEE, *APIS HENSHAWI* COCKERELL, FOUND IN GERMANY.

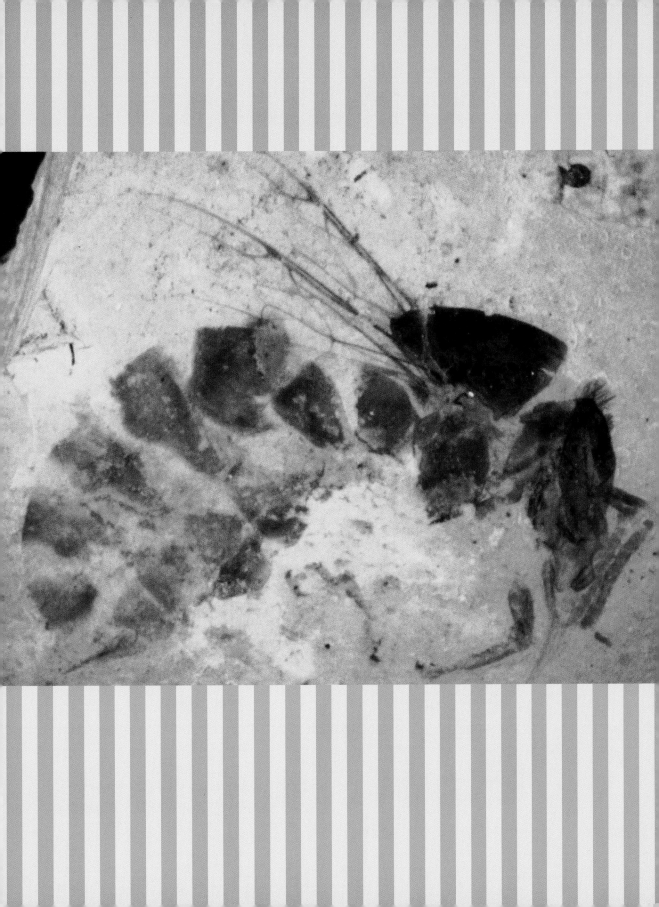

Bees had been evolving for millions of years before humans got involved, however. Today there are about 20,000 species.

Evolution

About 125 million years ago, the first bees evolved from wasps. Most wasps are hunters. They get the protein they need to feed their young by eating other insects. Unlike wasps, bees are vegetarians. They get all the protein they need from plants.

The first bees to evolve were solitary bees. They live alone, as most wasps do. The complex societies of honeybees and other social bees developed much later. As more complex species evolved, the simpler ones did not necessarily die out. Thousands of solitary bees still exist, along with partly social or semisocial bees, and the most advanced social bees.

Bees have evolved to feed on an immense variety of plants. They have adapted to live in almost every habitat, ranging from deserts to rain forests to the Arctic Circle. Wherever there are

ALTHOUGH IT LOOKS AS IF IT COULD HAVE BEEN ALIVE YESTERDAY, THIS BEAUTIFULLY PRESERVED BEE FOUND INSIDE A PIECE OF BALTIC AMBER IS ACTUALLY A LITTLE MORE THAN 45 MILLION YEARS OLD! THE AMBER ALSO CONTAINS BITS OF ANCIENT PLANTS, FUNGI, AND A SECOND BEE, WHICH IS UPSIDE DOWN AND TO THE LEFT OF THE FIRST BEE'S WING.

The Evolution of Bees

Millions of years ago

4 —— *Apis mellifera*
the common honeybee

tribe Apini —— **30**
first honeybees

family Apidae —— **100–105**
first pollen baskets

125 —— Apiformes first bees

superfamily Apoidea —— **140–142**   infraorder Aculeata
spheciform wasps —— **145–150**   first stinging wasps
bees' closest relatives   first flowering plants

190–200 — suborder Apocrita
first narrow "wasp waist"

origin of order —— **220–230**
Hymenoptera

first flying insects —— **340–350**

first insects —— **390–400**

Date estimates provided by
Dr. Michael S. Engel, University of Kansas

flowering plants, you will probably find bees. The biggest bees are more than an inch and a half long (4 cm), and the tiniest bees measure less than a tenth of an inch (2 mm).

Classification

More than one million kinds of insects have been discovered and named, and more remain to be found. Insects are classified into twenty-nine groups, or orders. Bees belong to the order Hymenoptera, which includes over 100,000 species of insects, including wasps and some ants. Most Hymenopterans have two pairs of wings and a pair of jaws for chewing or biting. Like butterflies, they grow by changing from an egg to a larva to a pupa to an adult through the process known as metamorphosis. Within this order, bees belong to the superfamily Apoidea. All bees depend on flowers for food. They have fuzzy, branching body hairs to catch pollen and special places on their hind legs or abdomen to carry it home.

The bee superfamily contains several families. Most contain only solitary bees. One family, called Apidae, includes most of the semisocial and social bees. Apidae, in turn, contains groups called tribes. These tribes include bumblebees, orchid bees, stingless bees, and honeybees. Within the honeybee tribe are several species, which are divided into different subspecies or races. One species, *Apis mellifera*, not only contains most types of bees used in beekeeping, but also the varieties known as killer bees.

Solitary Bees

Solitary bees live their lives entirely alone. These bees do not make and store honey, but they do gather nectar and pollen. Most solitary bees dig their nests underground. Others dig into branches, stems, or fruit. Some build nests in small holes such as nail holes. Some, called cellophane bees, line their nests with a liquid that hardens into clear sheets.

Each female solitary bee makes her own nest from leaves, stems, chewed plant fibers, or mud, depending on the species of bee. She puts some pollen into each individual cell. She lays one egg in each cell, then closes the cell, leaving enough food with each egg to last until the baby is full grown. This is called mass provisioning. By the time the grown bees emerge from the nest, their mother is dead. The vast majority of bee species live this way, never seeing their own offspring.

Though solitary bees do not share the work of making nests, some show hints of social behavior. Hundreds or thousands of sweat bees will build their nests close together, making it hard for an invader to sneak up on them. And some species in this family share tunnel entrances, although they still dig separate cells in the ground for their own eggs.

Bumblebees

Some bees work together, but have less complex social arrangements than honeybees. A good example is bumblebees. There are fifty known species of bumblebees in North America, and many more in South America, Europe, Asia, and North Africa. These fuzzy, black-and-yellow bees are a familiar sight in gardens. Their large size, bright colors, and loud buzzing make them hard to miss.

Though most bumblebees live underground, they do not dig their own nests. Instead, they search for existing holes or tunnels, such as abandoned mouse nests. Some bumblebees nest aboveground under a tuft of grass, in roofs, or in old furniture or bales of hay.

When a young bumblebee queen finds a good nest, she builds a large mound of pollen in the center of a round inch-wide burrow and lays her eggs on it. She then covers the mound with a wax roof. When the larvae hatch, they start eating the pollen that she left them. But the queen also opens the wax covering to feed them nectar, or a mixture of nectar and pollen. She also spends hours lying on the eggs to warm them like a nesting bird.

The larvae spin cocoons, turn into pupae, and emerge as adults. Though all are females, none mate or reproduce. Instead, they become workers and help their mother tend her next batch of eggs. The earliest workers are small because they are fed by the queen alone, but as later groups are fed by workers, they grow bigger. The workers help the queen build new cells on top of empty cocoons and cells. Empty cells are used to store nectar and pollen. Because the queen now has helpers, she can stop foraging. The family eventually grows to a few hundred bees, all working together.

Near the end of the breeding season, the colony produces breeding males and queens. Unlike male honeybees, male bumblebees gather their own food. Indeed, most male bumblebees leave the nest when they are two to four days old and never return. They live for only one to three months.

Bumblebee queens develop from the same eggs as the worker bees. Their future depends on what they are fed. In order to grow ovaries large enough to lay eggs, female bees must eat large amounts of pollen and nectar. The new queens help in the nest until it is time for them to mate. A young queen will go

A BUMBLEBEE'S BACK IS COVERED WITH YELLOW POLLEN.

outside to mate, then return home to fatten up for hibernation. Only young queen bees can store the fat needed to hibernate until spring. Her brothers, worker sisters, and mother will not survive the winter. Alone, the young bumblebee queen searches for a place to hibernate underground. In the spring, she lays her eggs and starts a new family.

Orchid Bees

The most brightly colored bees are the tropical and subtropical orchid bees. The 175 species of orchid bees range in color from green, red, blue, purple, gold, or red, to black and yellow, like the bumblebees, their close relatives. Orchid bees are considered semisocial, but in a different way from bumblebees. Unlike bumblebees or honeybees, orchid bees are communal, which means that several unrelated bees share a nest. But each orchid bee builds its own egg cells and raises its young alone. The same nest may remain in continuous use by different bees for several years.

Orchid bees live only in warm climates from Mexico to South America, so they are specially adapted to tropical plants. Some have tongues twice as long as their bodies in order to reach deep into those flowers.

Because tropical forests contain such diverse plants, orchid bees sometimes need to fly many miles to find flowers of the same species. Without orchid bees, many rare orchids would not be pollinated, and those varieties would die out. Many orchid bees follow a set route over great distances to regularly visit their favorite flowers. They have been known to fly as far as 30 miles (50 km) in search of certain flowers.

Many orchids attract bees with fragrant oils instead of nectar or pollen. When orchid bees feed on these oils, a pollen bundle called a pollinium sticks to the bee and releases pollen when it reaches another orchid. Orchid bees also gather a sticky sap called resin, which hardens when it dries. They use the resin to line the walls of their nests, or to seal the entrances to their hive at night.

Stingless Bees

Stingless bees live in warm parts of South America, southern Africa, and southeastern Asia. Some build large colonies with 80,000 workers. Other species have just a few hundred or a few thousand bees per colony.

Stingless bees make and store honey in wax combs, like honeybees. Before people brought honeybees to the Americas from Europe, the ancient Mayans of Mexico and Central America kept hives of stingless bees. Some people in South America still raid wild stingless beehives for honey, even though they may find only enough to fill a small gourd.

Because stingless bees do not have working stings, they have developed other ways to defend themselves. Some produce poisonous chemicals that burn attackers. Others attack the eyes, nose, and ears of an animal stealing their honey until it runs away. Some stingless bees bite so fiercely that their jaws stay fastened even when the rest of their body is pulled off, leaving the head behind.

Stingless bees often build hives in hollow trees using wax and plant glues such as resin. Their cells are stacked in layers separated by stiff poles, like a parking garage, and some are built upward in a continuous spiral. When the bees reach the top, they start filling cells with eggs or nectar again at the bottom, reusing cells from which young bees have already hatched.

Stingless bees have special ways to communicate with each other. Some species mark a food source with a strong scent that

A MASON BEE BUILDS A MUD NEST (FAMILY MEGACHILIDAE, GENUS CHALICODOMA).

A MINING BEE FEEDS ON A MARIGOLD (FAMILY ANDRENIDAE, GENUS ANDRENA).

ORCHID BEES DISPLAY
THEIR BRILLIANT COLORS
(FAMILY APIDAE, GENUS
EUGLOSSA).

A LEAFCUTTER BEE BUILDS ITS NEST FROM LEAVES (FAMILY MEGACHILIDAE, GENUS
MEGACHILE).

guides other bees to their hive. The odor comes from a chemical produced by a gland in the head. Chemical signals such as these are called pheromones. Some species even mark a path from the hive to the food by leaving pheromones on plants along the way. Other stingless bees lead their sisters to food by flying along with them. Some stingless bee species communicate by sound. They make loud noises that indicate how far away the food is by how long each burst of sound lasts.

Honeybees

Honeybees are the only types of bees in which an entire colony can survive severely cold winters. This is why they store honey. Unlike most bees, which gather food only to meet their daily needs and those of their young, honeybees must build a vast surplus for the winter. In cold climates, the bees in a single hive may eat more than 55 pounds (25 kg) of honey during wintertime. They do not hibernate, but instead cluster together in a ball and shiver their wing muscles to keep warm. Together, they create as much heat as a 40-watt lightbulb.

Starting out with a full force of workers in the spring gives honeybees a big advantage. While other bees are still building nests and raising their young, thousands of adult honeybees are already collecting nectar and pollen. This extra few weeks with the spring flowers is the secret to building up a store of honey. During the entire rest of the year, they eat almost as much as they collect.

Honeybees first evolved at least 30 million years ago in or near what is now India. Just one species arose outside the tropical forests of southern Asia: *Apis mellifera*. This species evolved in Africa, gradually developing the ability to withstand colder and colder climates as it spread across Africa and Europe. This is why it is the only species that can survive cold winters. Although its natural range for millions of years was confined to Africa, Europe, and parts of Asia, it was brought to the Americas and Australia by beekeepers and remains the primary beekeeping species worldwide. All other honeybee species still live only in tropical Asia. They include the dwarf honeybee, the giant honeybee, and the India honeybee.

Dwarf honeybees are just over a quarter of an inch (7 mm) long, and their colonies rarely contain more than five thousand bees. The bees make a single sheet of comb that hangs, unprotected, from a tree branch. On top of the comb they construct a flat platform. When one bee discovers a good source of food, it shows the others where to search by running in the direction of the food across the platform several times.

Because the comb is not enclosed safely in a hive, it could easily be eaten by birds or mammals, so the bees usually hide it from view inside a leafy bush. To keep ants from eating their honey, the bees coat the nearby twigs with propolis, a sticky sap that they gather from trees. Any ants that stumble upon the hive get stuck in the propolis and cannot escape.

Giant honeybees also do not build their combs in an enclosed hive, but they are so large and ferocious that they can drive away large animals. Giant honeybees are two-thirds to three-quarters of an inch long (17 to 19 mm), and their colonies contain over 20,000 workers. A few thousand attacking at once can kill just about anything. They do not bother to conceal their hives, although they do put them on cliffs or high in trees out of easy reach of animals and people.

Giant bees in mountainous regions such as the Himalayas have long, dark hair, which helps keep them warm. Because flowers bloom later in the year at high altitudes, bees sometimes move their hives up the mountainside to follow the blooming flowers.

Indian honeybees are similar to *Apis mellifera*. They are mild mannered, making them suitable for beekeeping. Indian honeybees, which live in colonies of six thousand to seven thousand workers, build several layers of comb inside a safe place, such as a hole in a tree. The only entrance into the hive is a small hole that keeps large animals out. Raiding insects are met at the entrance by a crowd of stinging guards.

Subspecies of *Apis mellifera*

As *Apis mellifera* honeybees spread across Africa and Europe, they encountered environments ranging from deserts to forests to freezing mountains. In each habitat, they changed to adapt to the local flowers and climate. In the process, they developed into separate races, or subspecies.

Italian bees first evolved in Italy, but they are now among the most popular bees kept by beekeepers around the world. With bright yellow bands across their abdomens, Italian bees are a familiar sight on flowers everywhere. They are gentle and rarely sting. Other European bees include **Carniolan bees**, which are even gentler than Italian bees and are gray or brown.

German dark bees are brownish black. Once popular with beekeepers, they are used less today because their tongues are too short to reach inside flowers such as clover, and they can be nervous and aggressive.

Caucasian bees are lead gray with long tongues and gentle dispositions.

African bees are generally smaller than European bees. They tend to be much more aggressive and to swarm, or start new colonies, much more often. Rapidly starting new colonies helped North African **Tellian bees** rebuild their numbers after droughts killed 80 percent of their colonies. **West African bees**

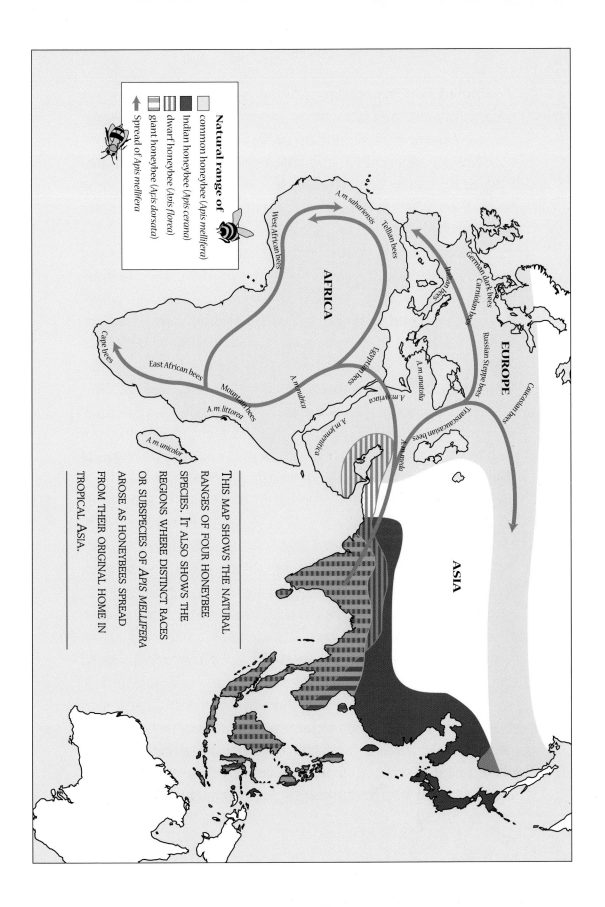

Natural range of

- common honeybee (Apis mellifera)
- Indian honeybee (Apis cerana)
- dwarf honeybee (Avis florea)
- giant honeybee (Apis dorsata)
- ↑ Spread of Apis mellifera

THIS MAP SHOWS THE NATURAL RANGES OF FOUR HONEYBEE SPECIES. IT ALSO SHOWS THE REGIONS WHERE DISTINCT RACES OR SUBSPECIES OF APIS MELLIFERA AROSE AS HONEYBEES SPREAD FROM THEIR ORIGINAL HOME IN TROPICAL ASIA.

AFRICA

EUROPE

ASIA

West African bees
A. m. sahariensis
Tellian bees
German dark bees
Carniolan bees
Italian bees
A. m. anatolia
Russian Steppe bees
Egyptian bees
A. m. syriaca
A. m. yemenitica
Transcaucasian bees
A. m. meda
Caucasian bees
Cape bees
East African bees
Mountain bees
A. m. nubica
A. m. littorea
A. m. unicolor

and the closely related **East African bees** are both extremely aggressive and can kill a large animal by attacking in large groups, earning their reputation as "killer bees."

Not all African bees are dangerous. The **mountain bee** lives in the mountains of Tanzania and is quite gentle. Its long hairs allow it to survive on chilly mountainsides 1 to 2 miles above sea level (1,500 to 3,100 m).

For centuries, people influenced bee evolution by breeding bees that produced more honey and were less likely to sting. Beekeepers have also transported bees around the world, where the bees interbred with the local races. For the most part, both the breeding and transporting of bees has led to a world filled with bees that are useful to humans. For example, North America, South America, and Australia became great places for bee-keeping after people filled these continents with gentle, hard-working strains of *Apis mellifera*. But human intervention can also cause problems. There is no better example than the spread of African "killer bees" throughout much of the Americas.

Killer Bees

In the 1950s, beekeepers in Brazil were having a hard time. Honeybees that did well in Europe could not handle the tropical climate of South America. Because Brazil's climate is more like that of Africa than of Europe, Warwick Kerr, a scientist at the University of São Paulo, reasoned that bees from Africa would thrive in Brazil. He knew that African bees are much more aggressive than European bees. Kerr thought that if he bred African bees along with European bees, he could keep the best traits of both, creating a new strain that would thrive in Brazil's hot climate but that would not attack people. In 1956, he shipped some African queens to Brazil. He kept them carefully guarded so that they would not escape and breed dangerously with local bees. But in 1957, they escaped.

The African bees quickly built hives in the wild and multiplied. They also took over beekeepers' hives. When an African bee mates with a European queen, that queen's offspring develop all of the African bees' worst qualities. Brazilian hives were soon filled with dangerous "Africanized" bees. It became unsafe to keep a hive near a house or even a road, because the bees might attack and even kill nearby people or animals.

What makes Africanized bees dangerous is that they attack by the thousands. They are easily provoked, often becoming aggressive because of sudden movements that European bees would simply ignore. A single sting from an Africanized bee is no more dangerous than that of a European bee. But when an Africanized bee stings, it releases an alarm chemical, or pheromone, that stimulates hundreds of other bees to join the assault. Once roused, a crowd of Africanized bees will continue attacking for hours.

Because African bees are fast flyers and because they move and build a new hive, which is called swarming, about every six weeks (compared to a few times per year for European bees), they have spread quickly since their escape from Kerr's hives. By 1980, they were living throughout South America. By 1990, they had entered the United States. By 2000, they had reached Arizona, New Mexico, Nevada, and Texas. Fortunately, cold weather in other parts of the country should keep them from spreading much farther. But Africanized bees have already caused problems. During a drought in 2000, when the desert plants could not provide the killer bees with food, they moved into cities such as Phoenix, Tucson, and Los Angeles. Simply running a lawn mower within one hundred feet of a hive can trigger an attack.

Africanized honeybees, or "killer" bees, are far more aggressive than other honeybees.

Africanized bees pose a major threat to beekeeping in North and South America. More than half of all Brazilian beekeepers have already given up, and those still working collect much less honey than they used to. Possibly the biggest problem caused by Africanized bees is that they cannot be used to pollinate crops. Colonies of killer bees cannot very well be set loose in fields full of farmworkers and animals. Without bee pollination, crop production could drop drastically.

3　Bee Bodies

Bees contain an amazing number of specialized tools in their tiny bodies. If the military tried to build a helicopter that could perform all of a bee's functions, the equipment required would probably weigh the helicopter down so much that it could not fly.

Unlike humans, bees have no bones. Like all insects, they have a hard shell that protects the soft, wet stuff inside. The body of a bee is made of three main parts: the head, the thorax, and the abdomen. All insects are composed of these three sections, which look like three separate shells connected by a narrow, flexible tube.

The Head

The front section, the head, contains the brain, eyes, and mouth. The head also supports the two antennae, sensitive feelers that bees use to hear, feel, smell, and taste.

AN AFRICANIZED HONEYBEE FEEDS ON A FLOWER. THE POLLEN BASKETS ON ITS LEGS ARE FILLED WITH YELLOW POLLEN.

Mouth. Bee's mouths are not at all like those of people. Instead, they have a set of clawlike mandibles, which function like a pair of jaws or pliers. Ridges on the mandibles help bees to grip and cut. Bees use their mandibles when fighting, chewing food, and shaping wax to build the hive. Mandibles are versatile enough to drag garbage out of the nest or to feed a baby larva.

Bees also have a tubelike proboscis, which is like a long straw with a tongue inside. It allows bees to poke deep inside a flower and suck out nectar. The proboscis folds up into a Z shape and can be tucked below the mouth. When unfolded, two sections form a stiff tube around the tongue, or glossa. The tongue itself is very hairy. It contains a spongelike tip that can

A HONEYBEE EXTENDS ITS TONGUE FROM ITS PROBOSCIS.

absorb liquid, such as water or nectar, and a narrow tube that carries liquids through the tongue into the mouth. Liquids sucked up through the tongue can be transferred to the tongue and stomach of another bee or into a storage cell.

Eyes. Bees have five eyes. Three are just tiny dots called ocelli arranged in a triangle on the top of the head. The ocelli cannot detect shapes, but they can measure the brightness of the sky. Bees may use them to check which way is up, or whether it is day or night.

The other two eyes are much larger than the ocelli. They are called compound eyes because they are made of many smaller eyes. Each compound eye contains thousands of separate lenses, or facets, each pointing in a slightly different direction. No one facet can see much by itself. But together they form a picture consisting of thousands of separate dots. This picture is not as sharp as that made by a human eye, but a bee's eye is much lighter, which is very important for a flying creature. Bees (and most other insects) have compound eyes because a human-type eye would weigh more than the rest of a bee's body.

Bees cannot see the color red, but they can see colors that are invisible to humans. People cannot see ultraviolet light—the invisible rays that cause sunburn—but bees can. Many flowers have patterns visible only to creatures that can see ultraviolet light. For instance, a flower may appear plain yellow to us, but to a bee, this same flower has lines on the petals pointing to a dark spot in the center. This pattern guides the bee to the flower's nectar and pollen.

Bees' eyes can also detect polarized light which lets them see invisible patterns in the sky that reveal where the Sun is even when it is hidden by clouds. This is important because bees use the Sun to find their way around.

Bees' eyes help with navigation in yet another way. Between

each facet are tiny hairs. As these hairs are blown from side to side, they measure how fast the wind is blowing and in which direction. If these wind-sensing hairs are removed from bees, the wind blows them off course. Bees have no sense of direction without them.

Antennae. Bees use their antennae to smell, hear, feel, and taste. Bees smell most things about as well as we do, but they are ten to one hundred times more sensitive to the odors that help them find food, such as flower scents. Bees can also smell some things that we cannot, such as carbon dioxide and water vapor.

Bees have three different sets of "ears": one at the base of their antennae, another at the joint where their antennae bend, and a third in the legs. These organs can hear only the few sounds that bees use to communicate. To all other sounds, bees are deaf. To humans, the constant buzzing and bustling of thousands of close-packed bodies would turn the hive into a blur of meaningless sound. To bees, the hive is silent except for the few sounds that are important to them, such as sounds made by the queen or by foragers telling where to find food.

In addition to feeling, smelling, and hearing, bees' antennae can taste. Bees also taste with the tip of their proboscis and their feet. As they crawl over a flower, they can probe for food with many different "tongues" at once.

The Thorax

The middle section of a bee's body contains everything it needs to get around—legs, wings, and the muscles to power them. Also, the entire thorax is covered with pollen-catching hair.

Legs. The thorax contains three segments, each with one pair of legs. At the end of each leg are a sticky pad and two curved, hooklike claws. The claws allow bees to cling to soft flower petals and even to hang upside down. The sticky pads are like suction cups that let bees grip smooth surfaces from any angle. Between the claws and the pads, bees can climb on almost anything.

Though all six legs have hairs for collecting pollen, each pair of legs is slightly different. The front legs have a notch in one joint that is especially adapted to cleaning the antennae. The

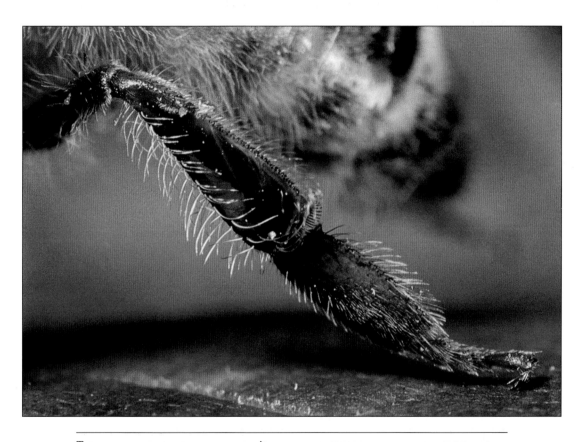

THE UPPER SECTION OF A HONEYBEE'S HIND LEGS CURVE INWARD LIKE A SPOON TO FORM A "POLLEN BASKET." STICKY WADS OF POLLEN MIXED WITH NECTAR OR WATER ARE PACKED IN A TIGHT BALL AND HELD IN PLACE BY SPIKY HAIRS.

bee puts an antenna in the notch and pulls it through to scrape it clean. The middle legs are covered with brushlike hairs for removing pollen from the body. These legs are also used to move pollen from the front legs to the rear legs for storage. The rear legs contain pollen baskets, where pollen is stored and carried. These "baskets" are actually indented areas that hold onto pollen in the same way that the bristles on a hairbrush grip hairs.

The pollen baskets are on the outside of the rear legs. On the inside of the rear legs are a row of combs and a rake, which scrape pollen off the legs and transfer it to a press—a joint in the rear leg that squeezes the pollen tightly before it is packed onto the pollen basket. A bee returning to the hive from gathering pollen will have a brightly colored blob on each rear leg. You can often tell what flowers or trees a bee has been to by the color of the pollen it is carrying.

Bees also use their pollen baskets to collect propolis, a sticky resin that they use to plug holes and glue things together in the hive. Bees snip off a glob of propolis sticking to a plant bud with their mandibles, then pass it backward from leg to leg. At home, other bees remove the propolis with their mandibles and set to work patching the hive.

Wings. All species of bees have two pairs of wings. The back wings of bees have a row of tiny hooks that attach to the front wings, allowing both wings to flap together.

Bees' flight is controlled by big muscles inside the thorax. The bee squeezes its entire thorax flat from the inside, causing the wings to flap. This allows the wings to beat much faster—up to 300 beats per second—than if they had their own tiny muscles. Honeybee foragers fly at an average rate of 15 miles per hour (24 km per hour). To fuel this incredible effort, worker bees stuff themselves with honey before leaving the nest, then digest it gradually over the course of the day.

The rear section of a bee, the abdomen, contains organs for digestion, reproduction, and wax making, along with the heart and the sting. The abdomen is made of seven segments, each with two armorlike plates connected by a stretchy membrane. This lets the whole abdomen expand when the bee fills up on nectar, water, or honey.

Bees have two stomachs, one to digest food and one to store it. To carry its load of nectar, a bee sucks the liquid into its mouth through the proboscis. A tube called the esophagus carries the food from the mouth to the stomach. But just before the food reaches the stomach, it enters an expandable bag called the crop, or honey, stomach. A valve keeps the liquid from going any

A HONEYBEE RAISES ITS ABDOMEN, EXPOSES ITS NASANOV GLAND, AND FANS IT WITH ITS WINGS. THE FLOATING SCENT ATTRACTS OTHER BEES.

farther into the real stomach, where it would be digested. When the crop is full, it takes up most of the abdomen. After the bee returns home, it can squeeze its abdomen and squirt the nectar back out of its mouth, undigested. Every drop of honey in every honey jar was once swallowed and regurgitated by a bee.

When bees do allow food into their real stomach and digest it, the wastes pass into the rectum. A bee's rectum can also stretch and expand. A bee will never release its waste inside the hive; it always waits until it flies outside. In places with cold winters, bees hold their waste in for months until it is warm enough to go outside.

SMALL PLATES OF FRESHLY MADE WAX EMERGE FROM THE GLANDS BENEATH THE ABDOMEN OF A BEE.

Head of Worker Honeybee

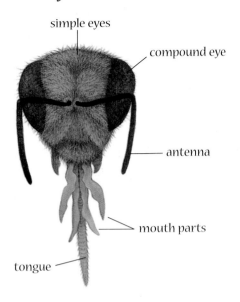

simple eyes

compound eye

antenna

mouth parts

tongue

Worker Honeybee Organs

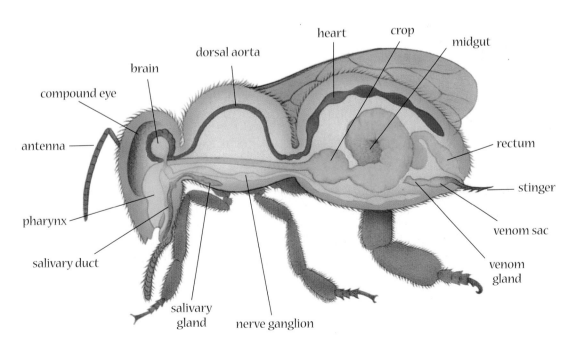

brain

dorsal aorta

heart

crop

midgut

compound eye

antenna

rectum

stinger

pharynx

venom sac

salivary duct

venom gland

salivary gland

nerve ganglion

A bee's heart is located near the rear of the abdomen. It pumps blood to the head through a tube called the aorta. Other muscles push the blood through the body and back to the abdomen. The blood does not flow through veins, as in humans, but simply floats around in the hollow body cavity.

Glands

Within the three main body sections, honeybees have several glands, organs that produce chemicals. These chemicals are used to digest food, make poison for the sting, create odors that send signals to other bees, make wax, and produce royal jelly, the special food for larvae and the queen.

All of the wax needed to make honeycomb is produced by the bees' bodies. To make wax, worker bees eat as much honey, pollen, and nectar as they can. Then they wait for their bodies to convert the honey into wax. The wax oozes out of four pairs of glands on the bottom of bees' abdomens. The wax comes out as a liquid and hardens into tiny flakes. The workers scrape off these flakes with their legs and chew them with their mandibles before adding the new wax to the comb.

One of the most powerful odors that a bee can produce comes from the Nasonov, or scent, gland. When a bee wants to guide other bees back to the hive, to water, or to a patch of nectar-rich flowers, the bee raises its abdomen, uncovers this gland, and fans it with its wings. The breeze blows the strong-smelling chemicals away through the air. When these pheromones reach other bees, they follow the odor to its source.

Other pheromones used for communication include the alarm scent released when bees sting. This pheromone tells other bees to join in the attack. A milder alarm scent is released from the mandibular glands in the head. In younger bees, these same mandibular glands, located at the base of the antennae, produce the royal jelly needed by baby larvae. A tube connects this gland to the mandibles, which allows bees to pass out food whenever they want.

The poison gland produces venom for the sting. The poison is stored in a small bag surrounded by muscles. When the muscles tighten, venom is squeezed out of the bag and through the hollow sting into the victim.

The Sting

The sting itself has two needlelike points called lancets. Honeybee lancets have barbs on them, so that once they go in, they cannot be pulled out. When a honeybee flies away after stinging, the sting is torn from its abdomen, and the bee dies. The entire sting is left behind, which continues to pump poison into the victim for up to a minute.

In most stinging insects—including many kinds of bees—the sting is not torn off. Bumblebees, for instance, can sting as many times as they want. Solitary bees would gain nothing by stinging an enemy if they died in the process, so their stings don't have barbs either. But honeybee colonies are better off sacrificing a few of their forty thousand or more members to make sure the rest are protected. But losing the queen would create a crisis for the hive, so her sting does not tear loose. Her poison sac holds two to three times as much venom as that of a worker bee, allowing her to sting repeatedly. However, a queen uses her sting only in fights with rival queens. Drones (male bees) have no sting.

To other insects and small animals, bee venom is deadly. People who are allergic to bee venom can die from a single sting. But for most people, bee stings are painful but not dangerous. Some can even get stung hundreds or thousands of times

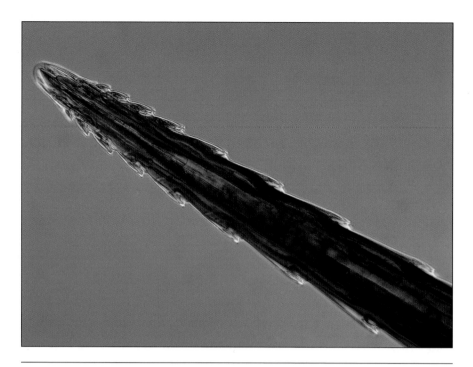

A WORKER BEE'S STING HAS BARBS THAT MAKE IT STICK INSIDE THE FLESH OF ITS
TARGET. WHEN THE BEE FLIES AWAY, THE STING TEARS FROM ITS BODY, KILLING THE BEE.

and survive unharmed. One person survived 2,243 bee stings—
a record few would wish to challenge.

Caste Differences

Among the truly social bee species, workers, drones, and queens
all have specialized features for their different tasks. Drones
have only one purpose in life: to mate with queens. Since
drones do no other work, they do not need the tools workers
use to gather food and tend the hive. They lack glands for producing wax, royal jelly, and the Nasonov scent. Drones have
only a tiny honey stomach, their proboscis is too short to reach

inside flowers, and they have no pollen-collecting hairs on their legs. However, they fly and see better than workers. This helps them spot a queen on her one mating flight and race to catch her.

Drones have special claws for grasping a queen in midair to mate. After a drone delivers the sperm that the queen needs to fertilize her eggs, its penis breaks off with a loud snap and stays inside the queen. The drone then dies, but its sperm will produce thousands of bees, making its life a success.

The queen's body is the most specialized of all. It is a virtual egg-laying machine. Her huge ovaries produce enough eggs to keep the hive bustling with thousands of workers. A single queen may produce more than a million eggs. Her reproductive equipment also includes a spermatheca, which stores the sperm acquired from the drones during mating. Each queen makes just one brief mating flight, in which she mates with up to five drones. During that flight she collects enough sperm to fertilize all the eggs that she will lay for the rest of her life. The spermatheca holds up to seven million sperm. When the supply of sperm finally runs out, after two to four years, the workers (or the beekeeper) will replace the queen.

As each egg passes from the ovary down a tube called the oviduct, the queen can release a small amount of this stored-up sperm to fertilize it. Fertilized eggs become worker bees; unfertilized eggs become drones.

Worker bees have smaller ovaries. They can sometimes lay eggs, and some of these eggs even hatch. But since workers cannot mate, their eggs are never fertilized. This means worker bees can produce only drones, which is why every hive needs a queen to survive.

4 A Bee's Life

A honeybee colony is a single family with one mother and forty thousand or more children. Except for a few hundred male drones, it consists entirely of workers, who are all female, and a single queen, the mother of them all.

The Birth of a Bee

Every worker begins its life in the same way: the queen lays an egg in an empty cell. First, however, the queen inspects the cell thoroughly. She will lay an egg only if the wax walls are polished perfectly clean, which prevents disease. Fifteen to thirty workers prepare each cell.

Inside the egg, an embryo grows. Three days later, the egg hatches, and a grublike larva comes out. At first, the larva is fed nothing but royal jelly, the high-protein food that worker bees feed the queen. After three days, however, the larva is fed honey

THESE HONEYBEE PUPAE HAVE NEARLY FINISHED THE PROCESS OF METAMORPHOSIS AND WILL SOON EMERGE AS ADULTS.

and pollen instead. (The nurse bees continue feeding royal jelly only to the larvae they want to become queens.)

Larvae are fed almost constantly during their first five days after hatching. Each larva is visited about 1,300 times a day. At the end of its first week, 2,700 different workers may have checked on it.

After about a week, the larva fills its entire cell. Worker bees cover the cell with a wax cap. Then the larva squirts out a liquid from an opening below its mouth and smears the liquid on the walls around it. The liquid dries into a tough, papery cocoon. Inside the cocoon, the larva becomes a pupa. The pupa is white

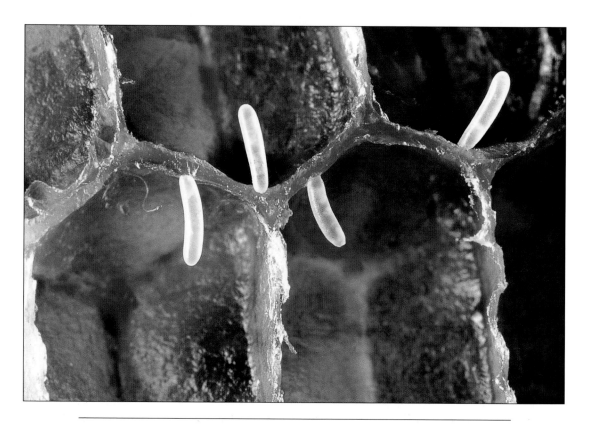

HONEYBEE EGGS IN THEIR WAX CELLS.

Stages of Honeybee Life

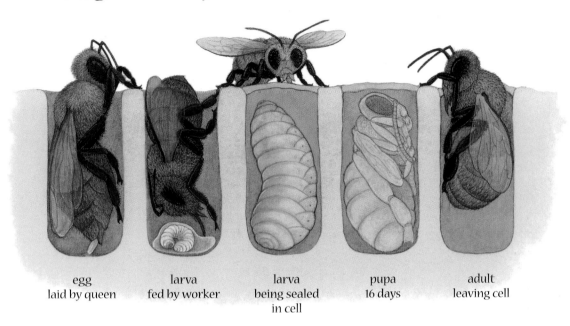

egg	larva	larva	pupa	adult
laid by queen	fed by worker	being sealed in cell	16 days	leaving cell

and is shaped like an adult bee. Over the next few days, the pupa slowly darkens. Eventually, it crawls out of its cell as an adult bee. Workers take about twenty-one days to grow from egg to adult. The larger drones take twenty-four days. Though they are even bigger, queens emerge in just sixteen days.

Worker Bees

From the day she emerges from the cell, a worker bee works. During her short life, she will rotate through many jobs. Her first task is to clean cells to prepare them for eggs, pollen, or honey. When her mandibular glands are able to produce royal jelly, she becomes a nurse bee. She feeds royal jelly to larvae so that they will grow, and to the queen so that she can produce eggs. Eventually, her mandibular glands stop working, and her wax glands take over. She then gorges on honey, nectar, and pollen, which her body converts to wax. Now her job is to build new cells on the comb and to cap cells when they are full of honey, pollen, or larvae ready to spin their cocoons.

When her wax glands stop working, she becomes an unloader, accepting nectar or pollen from foragers and putting it into cells. She may also spend some time as a fanner, blowing air through the hive to cool it. A worker bee may also take turns guarding in or around the hive entrance.

A YOUNG ADULT BEE THAT HAS JUST COMPLETED THE PUPAL STAGE EMERGES FROM ITS CELL FOR THE FIRST TIME.

Soon the worker bee begins practice flights, going out just far enough to learn to find her way back. At last, when she is about three weeks old, she is ready to begin foraging. This is by far the hardest job a worker will do. A single trip for nectar or pollen may take a bee more than 6 miles (10 km) from the hive. On each trip, a forager bee may visit several hundred flowers. Over her lifetime, a worker may make about four hundred foraging trips. In all that time, she will bring back enough nectar to make about one-twelfth of a teaspoon of honey.

Foraging makes terrible demands on a bee's body. As she flies on and on, scraping against flowers and struggling to free herself from spiderwebs, her wings become torn and frayed, and her hairs wear off. After about 500 miles (800 km) of flying, her body simply gives out. Unable to fly anymore, she falls to the ground and dies. Because she works at such a furious pace, her entire flying career may last perhaps three weeks. But during peak season, she may die after flying 500 miles (800 km) in just nine days.

Each bee works hard to produce a tiny amount of honey. That is why each colony needs tens of thousands of bees. Working together, they eventually gather enough to fill that jar of honey on your shelf, drop by laborious drop.

Drone Bees

Drones grow from eggs that are unfertilized. Though the queen can choose whether or not to fertilize an egg, she will lay a drone egg only in special drone cells. Because workers make these large drone cells, they control how many drone eggs the queen will lay. Occasionally, a worker bee will lay a drone egg, but since workers never mate, they can never create another worker.

A drone's life is ridiculously easy compared to a worker's. It spends most of its time in the hive, eating all it wants. In the late

THE HUGE EYES OF THE BRAWNY DRONE HELP IT TO SPOT QUEEN BEES ON THEIR RARE MATING FLIGHTS. THE DRONE'S BULGING THORAX MUSCLES HELP IT OUTRACE THE OTHER DRONES TO THE QUEEN.

afternoon, drones leave the hive to gather high in the air, looking for queens. Drones meet in the same places, year after year. No one knows how these spots are chosen or how the drones know where to go. Even though all the drones die in the fall, and an entirely new group emerges in the spring, they somehow always return to the same places.

When a young queen leaves her hive on a mating trip, she, too, heads for these drone meeting spots. When the drones see her, they race toward her, competing with one another for the chance to mate with her. This competition keeps weaker bees from mating with the queen, assuring that she will have strong, healthy offspring. As the drones chase after the queen, they form a cometlike trail behind her. The large number of drones ensures that her mating flight will be successful and provides decoys for birds. If the queen were eaten by a hungry bird during her mating flight, it would be a disaster for the hive. She is safer in a crowd because any bird passing by is more likely to make off with one of the more numerous drones.

At the end of the mating season, the drones are no longer needed. At this point, the worker bees refuse to let the drones eat any more food. The workers drag the drones to the hive entrance and throw them out. At first, the stronger drones try to barge their way back in. But they are outnumbered by unfriendly workers, who bite their wings. Banished from the hive, and unable to feed themselves, the drones grow weak and die.

Queen Bees

Queens are raised in cells that are even bigger than drone cells. Worker bees prepare queen cells before they swarm, which is when the queen and half the workers have to start a new hive. The workers may start about a dozen queens to make sure that at least one will remain to lay eggs—without a queen, the colony would die. If a colony's queen dies suddenly, any young female larva can be turned into a queen. Workers simply expand its cell and feed it royal jelly throughout the larva stage, instead of switching it to a diet of honey and pollen as they do when raising workers. Unneeded queen larvae are killed.

A queen's life consists of little more than laying eggs—up to two thousand per day. The eggs that she lays each day weigh as much as her entire body. To produce so many eggs, the queen must be fed royal jelly constantly. She is always surrounded by young bees that feed and groom her.

Honeybee Types

worker   queen   drone

Queens live much longer than workers do, sometimes for five or six years. But when the queen becomes too old to lay eggs, the royal treatment stops and the workers raise a new queen. Then about twelve workers or the new queen will fight and kill the old queen. No individual bee—even a queen—is more important than the colony.

Other Species

All bees pass through the same basic stages of development, changing from egg to larva to pupa to adult. But only social bees, such as honeybees, divide the hive's work among different castes of bees. With solitary bees, each female is both queen and worker, who does all the work of laying eggs and gathering food for the young drones.

A HONEYBEE QUEEN IS ALWAYS SURROUNDED BY WORKERS WHO FEED, CLEAN, AND LICK HER. THEY ARE DRAWN TO THE QUEEN'S CHEMICAL PHEROMONES. IF A QUEEN'S PHEROMONES ARE TRANSFERRED TO A MATCH STICK, WORKER BEES WILL SURROUND THE STICK AND IGNORE THE REAL QUEEN UNTIL SHE PRODUCES MORE PHEROMONES.

The thousands of bee species all behave differently, with widely varying approaches to food gathering and nest building. One important difference is in how bees spend the winter. Some spend the winter as pregnant adults and lay their eggs in the spring. Some lay their eggs in the fall and die. Then, their eggs hatch and grow into larvae. Other types of bees remain larvae all winter and finish maturing in the spring. Still others spend the winter as pupae. Some develop into adults, but remain in the cocoon until spring. The wide variety of bee species ensures that some type of bee will be available to pollinate plants at every point in the growing season.

5 Bee Talk

A bee enters the hive, its honey stomach bulging. Unloader bees gather around for a taste of the nectar it carries. The nectar is especially good—the sweetest brought in that day. The forager carries the smell of a new flower, one that must have just started producing nectar. Where did it come from? Is there more?

Other bees gather around the forager. In the darkness of the hive, they feel it with their antennae. The forager makes a short dash across the comb, then curves back to the right, making a half circle that ends up where it started. It makes the same short dash again—no more than an inch or two—then circles back, making another half circle, this time to the left. It repeats this over and over, making short runs and then circling back on alternate sides. During each straight run, it waggles its abdomen several times.

A RETURNING FORAGER EXCHANGES FOOD WITH ANOTHER BEE.
NOTE THE FORAGER'S BULGING YELLOW POLLEN BASKETS.

In less than ten seconds, the bees around it depart. The forager bee is quickly surrounded by other bees, and the dance continues. Now and then, one of the bees in the audience makes a brief sound. The dancing bee stops, gives the questioner a sample of its nectar, then continues to dance. More members of the audience leave and fly out of the hive. Fifteen minutes later they return with full loads of the same nectar.

How did they know where to go? All the directions that they needed were contained in this mysterious dance. Humans have known about the code language of bees only since the 1950s. But to bees, this code is nothing new. They have been communicating in this way for millions of years—long before humans even existed.

The dance language of honeybees is nothing short of astounding. It is easily the most complex language of any animal on Earth besides that of humans. But bees have many other ways to communicate as well, including sending messages by sound and smell.

The Language of Bees

Honeybees work together so perfectly that some people refer to the *hive mind*, as if a single brain controlled the actions of 40,000 individuals. When a colony needs to make a major change, such as raising new queens or swarming, many preparations must be made in advance. How does each bee know what to do?

Like many other animals, bees produce chemicals called pheromones that serve as signals to other bees. When a bee smells a particular pheromone, it stimulates behaviors such as giving food, mating, or attacking. Some pheromones are released automatically by the bee's body. Others are sent out only when the bee needs to send a message.

Because the queen is so important to the hive—she lays all the eggs for the entire colony—the main information that bees need to know at all times is that the queen is okay. If she dies, they must start raising a new queen immediately. Any fertilized egg can be turned into a queen but only within three days after the egg is laid. After three days the egg can only become a worker. With only worker eggs and no queen to lay more, there will be no chance to replace the queen. Without a queen to lay eggs, the entire colony will die.

When the queen dies, all the other bees in the hive know within about half an hour. They buzz around, clearly upset. Anyone observing the hive can tell that something is wrong. Within twenty-four hours, the bees start building large cells for the creation of a new queen.

To prevent workers from producing a new queen when the queen is still healthy, the queen's body constantly produces a mixture of pheromones known as queen substance. Worker bees lick the queen substance off the queen's body and pass it on to other bees until it spreads throughout the entire hive. As long as the workers keep receiving queen substance, they know the queen is alive and healthy.

Sometimes the hive becomes so crowded that some workers do not receive enough queen substance. When this happens, workers start raising new queens and prepare for swarming. During swarming, the old queen and half of the workers leave to start a new colony. Those worker bees who stay behind need a new queen. So, before the swarm leaves, several young queens are raised.

At any given moment, the beginnings of queen cells exist somewhere in the hive. As worker bees pass these cells, some will

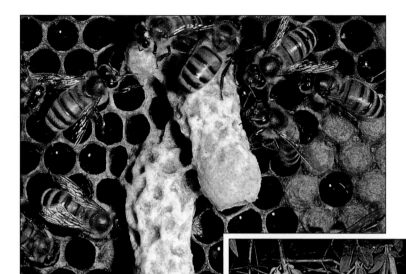

OVERSIZED QUEEN CELLS
HANG FROM THE COMB.
WORKERS MUST BUILD
THESE LARGE, PEANUT-
SHAPED CELLS TO RAISE A
NEW QUEEN.

WHEN BEES SWARM, OR
LEAVE THE HIVE TO START
A NEW COLONY, THEY
GATHER IN A CLUSTER
UNTIL A NEW HOME
IS FOUND.

PHEROMONE EXPERIMENTS

Most pheromones float through the air as odors, but queen substance must be physically passed from bee to bee. In one experiment, a fence was put into a hive to divide it into two parts. Air and odors could pass through the fence, but bees could not. On the side without the queen, worker bees could still smell her other pheromones, but because they were unable to receive queen substance, they quickly raised a new queen.

The experiment was repeated with a different fence that kept the bees on their own side, but that let them touch one another. This time, on the side without the queen, worker bees did not raise new queens. Instead, they acted as if everything was normal. As long as queen substance was being passed to them, they knew she was still okay.

Probably the main way that queen substance is spread around the hive is by exchanging food. In one experiment, just six bees from a hive of 24,600 adults were fed sugar syrup containing a radioactive marker. Within hours, this syrup had been passed on to thousands of other bees. By the next day, more than half the bees in the hive had the marker in their bodies. Incredibly, over 10,000 bees had received a portion of the food gathered by those six foragers.

add a little wax, and others will tear off a little wax. In this way, each is "voting" for or against swarming. Because not all worker bees receive the same amount of queen substance each day, they have different ideas about whether or not to swarm. When those adding wax outnumber those removing wax, the queen cell grows, and the colony is on the path toward swarming.

Sound

Bees also use sound to communicate. By vibrating their wing muscles with their wings folded up, bees can make a loud buzzing sound. Bees called scouts use one type of buzz to announce that it is time to swarm. Scouts search for new hive locations and then race through the hive, buzzing to raise the bees to depart. Forager bees create another kind of buzzing sound during the dances that tell other bees where to find food.

Bees' strangest use of sound is when they communicate with the queens that are still inside their wax cells. Normally, replacement queens do not emerge until the old queen has left with a swarm. When swarming is delayed by bad weather, the new queens must be prevented from coming out because otherwise the old queen will kill them. To check whether a new queen is about to emerge, the old queen buzzes in one long two-second note followed by several short notes. The noise vibrates throughout the comb. Young queens who are still in their wax cells respond with a series of about ten short buzzes. To prevent trouble, workers climb on the young queens' cells and shake them to keep the new queens trapped inside until the old queen has left.

Once the swarm leaves, the first queen to hatch often leads a second, smaller swarm, called an afterswarm. This can happen up to four times. In each case, unhatched queens are kept in their cells, using the same buzzing code. After the last swarm has gone, a new queen is put in charge of the hive. Because she does not want any other queens around, she uses this same buzzing sound to find unhatched queens, then kills them by stinging them through the cell wall. If any other queens do get out, they will battle to the death until only one queen remains.

Many animals, including mammals and insects, use pheromones. And many creatures send messages to each other using sounds. But no other animal, large or small, can match the dance language of bees.

The Round Dance

These are two basic forms of bee dancing. The simplest is the round dance. It is used only to tell of food sources very near to the hive. The dancing bee runs in small circles on the comb wall, reversing direction every one or two times. Since the hive is pitch-dark, the bees gather around the dancer and feel its movements with their antennae. Whenever a bee in the audience makes a short buzz, the dancer stops and gives that bee a sample of the food. The observers can also smell the nectar or pollen that the dancer is "advertising." If an observer likes the sample, it will fly out and find the flower that the nectar or pollen came from by its scent. On returning, this bee may dance, too. A really good food source will soon be advertised by several dancers.

The Waggle Dance

A sample of pollen or nectar alone is not enough to find food sources farther away from the hive. If the flower bed is more than a mile away, it could take bees hours to find it just using scent. For distant food sources, bees use the waggle dance. This incredible dance tells other bees both in what direction and how far away the food is. After observing this dance, a bee can fly right to a flower patch several miles away.

In the waggle dance, a forager bee makes a short run along the side of the comb and then circles back to the starting point. The bee then runs again in the same direction, this time circling back the opposite way from the first time. The forager repeats this figure eight over and over, sometimes for several minutes.

The direction of the run indicates the direction to the food source. But how can a bee show the direction along the ground by dancing on the side of a comb that is hanging straight down? Bees solve the problem by substituting vertical directions for horizontal ones, using the comb walls as a map. When people hang a map on a wall, up stands for north. For bees, up means toward the Sun. So if a bee wants to tell the other bees to fly toward the Sun, it runs upward. (Imagine running toward the twelve on a clock face.) The direction away from the sun is shown by running straight down (or toward six o'clock). Running up and to the right (or toward two o'clock) would indicate a 30-degree angle to the right of the Sun.

The dancer shows how far to fly by waggling her abdomen during this run. The number of waggles indicates the distance to the food: the more waggles, the farther away the food. For Italian honeybees, each waggle stands for about 65 feet (20 m). So, to an Italian honeybee, a run with five waggles means that the bee should fly 325 feet (99 m) from a hive in the direction indicated. Bees are born with the ability to understand the code of their particular subspecies. To an Egyptian bee, each waggle stands for about 40 feet (12 m). To a Carniolan bee, one waggle means a good 150 feet (45 m). An Egyptian bee raised in a Carniolan hive would fly the wrong distance after counting the waggles in a Carniolan dance.

Dancing is important because the best places to gather food change constantly. Many wildflowers bloom for only a few days each year. And some flowers release nectar only at certain times of the day. Even at the peak blooming time, flowers quickly run out of nectar and pollen after many bees and other insects have visited them. So scouts always keep searching for good sources of nectar, pollen, water, and propolis. Then they report their findings by dancing.

Waggle Dance

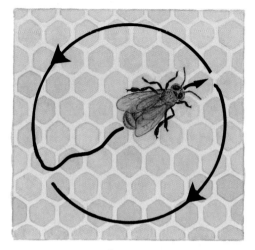

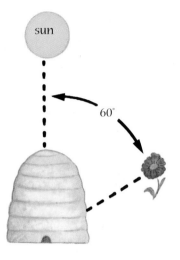

direction

distance

WORKER BEES GATHER AROUND A FORAGER THAT IS PERFORMING A WAGGLE DANCE. THE DANCE TELLS THEM WHERE THEY CAN FIND FOOD OR WATER.

But scouts must first decide whether a particular location is worth dancing about. One factor in whether they dance is how much interest unloader bees show in the food that they have brought back. If the nectar is very sweet, the scouts will be crowded by bees eager to unload it. If few bees accept the nectar, the scouts are less likely to dance.

Audience bees must also decide whether to go to the site advertised. Even if the nectar offered is very good, before flying off the bees might attend other dances to see if a closer source of food is available.

The person who first decoded the dance language of bees was an Austrian zoologist named Karl von Frisch. He was so amazed to learn that honeybees were literally talking in code that he performed numerous experiments to prove it. When he published his most important findings in 1946, many scientists didn't believe him. Some thought he was crazy. But in 1973 he earned a Nobel Prize for his work.

6 Honey Thieves

On the platform in front of the hive entrance, guard bees keep a watchful eye out for robbers. The guards smell each arriving bee carefully to make sure it belongs in the hive. If it doesn't, they pounce on it and sometimes kill it. Still, every now and then a bee from another hive tries to sneak in and steal honey.

The robber first checks the sides and back of the hive, trying to find a crack to squeeze through. In a well-tended hive, however, every crack is sealed tight. The robber returns to the front entrance and waits, patiently inching forward whenever the bees guarding the hive look away. But the guard bees almost always catch the intruder and throw it out. Experienced robbers, however, have many tricks for getting past guards. Indeed, some bees do no foraging at all. Instead, they spend all their time trying to sneak into neighboring hives. These old pros are often shiny black, because all their hair has been worn off wrestling with guards.

PEOPLE IN THE YUCATAN PENINSULA OF MEXICO COLLECT HONEY FROM A STINGLESS BEE COLONY.

When one of these crafty robbers approaches a hive, it lands quietly on the landing platform. If it is a hot day, a group of fanners crouches nearby, beating their wings to send a cool breeze through the hive. The robber joins them and starts fanning. When a suspicious guard comes to check, the robber keeps its head lowered and fans furiously. It does not even seem to notice that it is being examined. When the guard moves away, the robber creeps closer to the door, joining the next row of fanners. The guard returns, suspicious, but leaves the new fanner alone. Guards keep checking until the robber is no longer there—it has dashed inside the hive.

Some daring robbers actually pretend to *be* guards. The imposters stop to examine innocent worker bees returning to their own hive. The confused guards don't know what to do. Other robbers sneak in by joining a crowd of workers entering together. Still other honey thieves gather a load of pollen and carry it into another colony's hive. Once inside, they dump the pollen, fill up on honey, and carry it back to their own hive.

Neighboring bees are not the only animals who try to steal honey. Nowhere else in nature can such a glorious treasure of sweet, concentrated sugar be found. Gathering nectar from millions of flowers and storing it as honey allows honeybees to live through the winter. But the honey also makes them a target for hungry animals of every size. As honeybees evolved, they had to develop defenses against every possible attacker. Many found ways to hide or protect their wealth inside hollow trees or other enclosed areas. They also developed dangerous stings.

Animal Robbers

Bees must defend their colonies against many enemies. Bumblebees, which nest in the ground, must watch out for prowling

CROUCHING BY THE HIVE ENTRANCE, WORKER BEES FAN WITH THEIR WINGS TO SEND A BREEZE THROUGH THE HIVE.

badgers. For all bees, large wasps can be dangerous. They walk right into the hive, ignoring the guard bees hanging from their bodies. Wasps often raid early in the morning, when it is too cold for bees to be up and about, and then leave the hive with a bulging stomach full of honey. Wasps may also perch at the entrance and snip returning forager bees in half in order to eat their nectar-filled honey stomachs.

In South America, an animal called the kinkajou has earned the nickname "honey bear" (even though it is most closely related to the raccoon) because it eats so much honey. Though its long tongue can reach inside flowers, the kinkajou much prefers to let bees collect the nectar for it. Actual bears are an unstoppable enemy of bees. They are so strong that they can tear open a tree and eat an entire comb, wax and all. The

THE KINKAJOU, A NOTORIOUS RAIDER OF WILD BEEHIVES.

angry bees cannot sting the bears through their thick fur. Bears can also climb trees and attack the hives. When a black bear finds a collection of hives, it will stay nearby for weeks, eating the bee colonies one by one. Bears can do immense danger to the beekeepers' hives before anyone notices.

Many birds present a danger to bees because they can snatch flying bees out of the air. Even a small bird such as a fly-catcher can eat a tremendous amount of insects, especially if it hangs around a hive. A clever bird called the titmouse visits bee-hives during the winter, when the bees are inside resting. The titmouse taps near the hive's entrance with its beak, and when a sleepy guard bee comes to check on the noise, the bird eats it. The titmouse repeats this over and over until it is full. Toads sometimes make their home right under a hive and live for

A BEE-EATING BIRD SNAPS UP A MEAL.

months by gobbling up bees returning to the hive, their bellies full of sweet nectar. Skunks and opossums also like to snap up bees as they fly out of the hive.

In Africa and Asia, a particular pest is the honey badger, or ratel. These black-and-white skunklike mammals have thick, loose, rubbery skin that protects them from bee stings. Ratels will rip open hive after hive to feast on the honey.

To locate hives in the wild, ratels rely on a bird called the honeyguide. This small African bird loves to eat bee larvae and beeswax, but it cannot get inside the hive itself. So, when the honeyguide finds a beehive, it makes a loud noise to attract the attention of a honey badger. The bird will lead the honey badger miles through a forest to a beehive, chattering loudly all the way. When the ratel rips open the hive, the honeyguide is rewarded with a feast of unprotected grubs. Some people in Africa have also learned to follow honeyguides to hives. After stealing the honey, the people always throw the honeyguide a chunk of comb. They fear that if they do not, the next time the bird might lead them to a lion or poisonous snake.

Human Honey Robbers

People have been stealing honey in one way or another for thousands of years. Rock paintings in Europe and Asia dating back to 15,000 B.C. show people raiding wild hives. Other pictures depict angry bees surrounding people climbing ropes or ladders to carry away the honeycomb. Ancient paintings also show hunters using smoke to calm the bees, as people still do today. In many parts of Asia and Africa, raiding wild hives is still an important source of honey. In India, people collect honey from giant and dwarf honeybees, as well as Indian bees and *Apis mellifera*. In Africa, some people eat not only the honey but also

THE BEE-PROOF SHED

In his lively and entertaining book *A Hive of Bees*, John Crompton writes about a beekeeper who bought a "bee-proof" shed. In it he put all the honey produced by his bees—about four hundred pounds of it. The scent of all this honey attracted robber bees, and somehow one bee found its way in through a tiny crack. Other bees gathered around, all trying to squeeze into the shed. When the beekeeper returned, it was surrounded by a black cloud of bees.

He opened the door to find the shed completely full of bees. Though the bees managed to squeeze in, after filling up on honey they were too swollen to squeeze back out. So instead, the bees used their tongues to pass the honey out through narrow cracks to the bees outside. Drop by drop, they managed to remove every ounce of honey in the shed. An entire year's worth of honey was gone.

the wax and larvae. Bee larvae are very nutritious and are said to have a delightful taste.

Early Beekeepers

Early honey hunters in Europe, Asia, and Africa learned that if they did not destroy the entire colony, they could come back again later and take more honey. In Europe, people often climbed trees to carve a rear entrance to a beehive. While the bees were going in and out of a hole in the front of the tree, the robber could stealthily take a comb of honey from the back. This left the combs of eggs and larvae in the front undisturbed. To prevent other people from taking the honey from a particular hive, a person who found a good "bee tree" would mark the tree to claim it. In Europe during the Middle Ages, the owner would cut his mark on the tree trunk. He legally owned the honey and could pass it on to someone else in his will. Claiming and marking wild nests still continues in many parts of the world. In Oman, a person who finds a colony of dwarf bees living in a cave builds a small pyramid of rocks in front to claim it. In the Congo, Epulu pygmies tie a vine around a "bee tree" trunk. In South Africa, a wild bee colony might be the one possession that a Bushman passes on to his children.

Over time, people learned that they could get more honey by building artificial hives and raising their own. Pictures from 2400 B.C. in Egypt offer the oldest known evidence of beekeeping. The ancient Egyptians built wide, tubelike hives out of dried mud. Several of these hives could be stacked to form a wall, with the bee entrances all on one side. Beekeepers could open the back of the hives to remove honeycomb without being stung.

The ancient Greeks improved on this design, making larger hives out of clay. In the Roman empire, hives were made of clay, wooden boxes, hollow logs, woven wicker, or brick. But all had a narrow bee entrance at one end and a door at the back from which to remove honey and wax.

In most of Europe, beekeeping developed more slowly. During the Middle Ages, people still climbed trees to take honey from wild hives, or hung hollow logs from ropes for bees to move into. But even with these unsophisticated methods, in 1136 a single church in Novgorod, Russia, was able to collect 800,000 pounds of beeswax from its parish. It took half a million bee colonies to produce that much wax. The Catholic Church was by far the biggest user of wax in Europe. King Henry III of England kept 1,500 beeswax candles burning in St. Paul's Cathedral for a

BEEKEEPERS TODAY USE REMOVABLE FRAMES THAT GLIDE IN AND OUT OF HONEYBEE HIVES. THAT MAKES IT MUCH EASIER TO GET HONEY FROM THE HIVES THAN IT USED TO BE.

religious feast in 1243. People were often required to pay their taxes in beeswax. While the churches were filled with beeswax candles, beekeepers were forced to burn smelly, smoky candles made from animal fat.

Until just a few hundred years ago, many European beekeepers still had not figured out how to remove honey from hives without killing the bees. European bees were kept in a woven container called a skep, which had no doors for harvesting honey. To get at the honey, the beekeepers either held the skep under water to drown the bees or killed them with smoke from burning sulfur.

Modern Beekeeping

Several inventions and advances made it possible to remove honey from bee colonies without harming the bees too much. Most of these discoveries date from over a hundred years ago. Since then, beekeeping methods have changed little.

Removable Comb. Extracting honey from a wild hive is difficult. Bees attach the sides of the comb to the walls of the hive, and separate layers of comb are sometimes attached together. The comb has to be cut up to be removed.

Today, beekeepers use removable frames that slide in and out of the hive. Bees make comb by attaching wax to these frames. When frames were first introduced, bees glued them to the walls of the hive and to each other so the frames still had to be cut loose to remove the combs. An American beekeeper, the Reverend L. L. Langsroth, solved this problem after discovering what is called "bee space." In 1851, Langsroth observed that if he left a gap of precisely three-eighths of an inch between the combs, bees would not attach them together. Langsroth realized that this distance allowed just enough room for bees to crawl

BEES MUST EAT EIGHT POUNDS OF HONEY TO MAKE ONE POUND OF WAX. IT TAKES A LOT OF BEES TO DO THAT.

back-to-back on facing pieces of comb. If the space is any wider, the bees build another layer of wax cells connecting the combs. If the gap is narrower, they connect the combs together for strength. Only if there is room for two bees to work back-to-back, with no extra space, do the combs remain unattached.

Comb Foundation. Langsroth still needed to find a way for bees to build their comb inside his frames. In 1857, a German

A BEEKEEPER LIFTS A FRAME OF REMOVABLE COMB FROM A HIVE.

beekeeper, Johannes Mehring, found that if he put a flat piece of beeswax in the frame and pressed a pattern for comb cells into it, his bees would build a complete comb onto his foundation. The first foundations were made by pressing recycled beeswax between wooden patterns. Later, hot wax was poured into plaster molds. But the best method, invented in 1873, was to press the foundation wax between metal rollers. Wax foundation is still made this way, though printed sheets of plastic are also used.

An added benefit of using foundation is that all the cells can be the correct size for making honey. When bees make their own comb, they include several larger cells for raising drones. When there are fewer drone cells in the foundation, the bees raise fewer drones. Beekeepers prefer that because drones eat a lot of honey and do not make any.

Queen Excluders. Cells for storing honey, pollen, and worker eggs are all the same size, so even comb built on a man-made foundation may contain some of each. Beekeepers, however, want certain frames to contain only honey for easy removal.

An invention called a queen excluder allows beekeepers to keep some frames free of eggs. The queen excluder is simply a fence with holes just large enough to let worker bees through. The larger queen bee cannot get through to lay eggs in the fenced-off comb, but the workers pass back and forth, filling the frame with honey only. Queen excluders can be made by making holes in a sheet of metal or by laying carefully spaced wires across a frame.

Honey Extractors. Every time comb is removed from the hive, bees must consume much precious honey to get the energy to replace it. Bees eat more than eight pounds of honey to make one pound of wax. An 1865 invention called the honey extractor allows beekeepers to take the honey without destroying the comb. The tops of the wax cells are sliced off, and a machine spins the open comb to remove the honey. The empty comb is then put back into the hives. This means the bees can go right to work making more honey, instead of wasting time, food, and energy building new comb.

Smokers. People have used smoke to calm bees for centuries. No one is precisely sure why it works, but smoke will make a colony of bees rush to fill up with honey as if preparing to flee a fire. Even when their hive is opened, they will not fly out to attack. But simply waving a burning branch near a hive

A HONEY EXTRACTOR, OR CENTRIFUGE, SPINS FRAMES OF HONEYCOMB TO FORCE OUT THE HONEY.

A BEEKEEPER CALMS HIS BEES WITH A SMOKER BEFORE OPENING THE HIVE.

does not direct the smoke where a beekeeper wants it. In1873, a man named Moses Quinby invented a smoker that blows smoke directly into a hive. Beekeepers can now direct a puff of smoke exactly where they need it, until every bee is calm.

Over the hundreds of years that honeybees have lived with humans, the bees have changed very little. Their behavior is the same whether they live in artificial hives or in the wild. People provide sturdy, dry homes for bees, and although beekeepers steal some honey, they always leave enough for the bees to feed on over the winter. But while people need to get honey or beeswax, bees do not need people. A colony that escapes can do fine in the wild, and every year, many bee colonies do just that.

7 Threats to Bees

Bees get sick, just as people do. Because honeybees live in such close quarters, it is easy for a disease to spread throughout the entire colony. Occasionally, an epidemic devastates not just one colony but all the bees in an entire country. Such an epidemic spells disaster not only for bees and beekeepers, but also for farmers who depend on honeybees to pollinate their crops.

In the early twentieth century, nearly all the honeybees in Great Britain died in an epidemic called Isle of Wight disease, named for the island where it was first noticed. Today, bees in North America are facing a similar crisis. In the 1990s, the United States lost more than half of all commercially owned honeybees, and almost all of those living in the wild. People are still struggling to find a solution that will save the honeybees—and the $10 billion worth of crops per year that they pollinate.

A FUZZY BUMBLEBEE FEEDS ON A FLOWER.

Bee Diseases

A large number of diseases affect bees, including illnesses caused by bacteria, viruses, fungi, and parasites such as mites. Two of the worst bacteria to strike honeybees are American foulbrood and European foulbrood. American foulbrood kills bee larvae in their cells, usually right after they have spun their cocoons. When the larvae are ten to fifteen days old, they turn brown and decay, causing a foul odor that smells like fish or glue. Adult bees remove the dead larvae to keep the disease from spreading, but if it infests more than a hundred cells, the entire colony

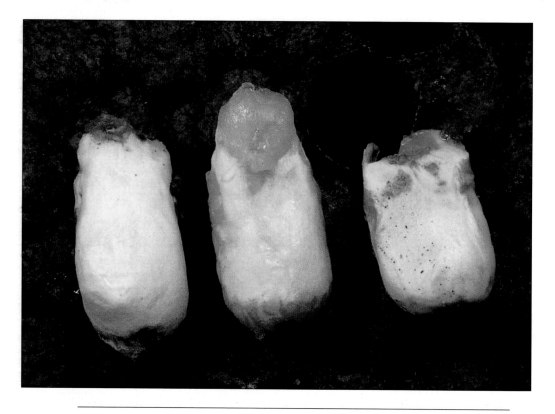

BEE LARVAE THAT HAVE BEEN STRICKEN WITH CHALK-BROOD FUNGUS.

will likely die. European foulbrood strikes four-to-five-day-old larvae. Foulbrood was the single biggest bee problem in North America for most of the twentieth century. To prevent its spread, diseased bee colonies must be killed and their hives burned. In the early 1930s, more than one in twenty hives in New York State had to be burned. Today, foulbrood is still found in about one out of every hundred hives.

A common bee virus is sacbrood, which causes a larva's skin to harden. The inside of the larva then becomes liquid, creating a balloonlike sac. Even more dangerous is a virus called paralysis. Bees struck with paralysis tremble, are unable to fly, and their abdomens swell. Thousands of sick bees may crawl along the ground or up grass stems before dying. Chalk-brood and stone-brood are caused by a fungus that kills larvae, which first turn fluffy, and then harden. Both chalk-brood and stone-brood are widespread in Europe and North America.

Parasites are animals that live and feed on other animals. The worst bee parasites are mites, tiny creatures related to ticks. Just as ticks cling to people and animals and suck their blood, mites live as parasites in or on bees. More than forty kinds of mites attack honeybees. In the 1940s, two types of mites nearly destroyed beekeeping in Great Britain. In the 1980s, these same mites invaded the United States, causing a crisis for bees, beekeepers, and farmers that is still going on.

The Mite Crisis

The reddish brown Varroa mite is the only bee mite big enough to see with the naked eye. It clings to the bee's body and lives by sucking the bee's blood. The mites spread from adult bees to larvae and kill an entire colony in six months to two years if not stopped.

The other problem mite is called a tracheal mite, because it lives inside bees' tracheas, or breathing tubes. This mite lays eggs and multiplies there, making it hard for the bee to breathe. During the summer, honeybees can survive with tracheal mites because workers live for just a few weeks, and the mites do not have time to multiply enough to do great damage. But in the winter, bees live much longer. As the bees huddle together through the long winter months, the mites multiply and spread throughout the colony.

With their breathing tubes choked with mites and their bodies weakened, infested bees cannot summon the energy to shiver. Because this shivering is their sole source of heat, the entire colony can die during a cold winter.

In 1996, many people found their gardens eerily silent after an unusually cold winter in the United States. Normally their flowers would be buzzing with bees, but that year, none came. Over the winter, more than half the nation's bees had died. In some states, the death toll reached 80 percent. Many beekeepers were put out of business.

Besides killing bees, the mites pose a serious threat to American agriculture. More than ninety crops depend on bees to pollinate them, including apples, oranges, almonds, tomatoes, raspberries, watermelons, cucumbers, and zucchini. In 1996, beekeepers whose bees had survived scrambled to meet the needs of the nation's farms, sending trucks all across the country.

Modern Farming Methods

The real danger to American bees is greater than any one disease. Modern farming methods make it much easier for bee diseases to spread. In the past, farms were small and were surrounded by wild land, where many kinds of wild bees could live. Today,

A DISEASED BEE WITH SMALL BROWN VARROA MITES VISIBLE ON ITS BACK AND NECK. VARROA MITES ARE PARASITES THAT LIVE AND FEED ON BEES, WEAKENING THEM AND SPREADING DISEASES.

miles and miles of land are planted with a single crop, and there is often no brush, trees, or wild grasses for wild bees. These huge farms and orchards are too big to be pollinated by the few wild bees that remain. And since their single crop blooms all at once, there is no food for the bees for the rest of the year. To pollinate

BEEKEEPERS IN UTAH PREPARE TO TRANSPORT THEIR HIVES.

their crops, giant farms must pay beekeepers to truck in honeybees. More than a million bee colonies are rented by farmers
each year.

Moving so many bees to one place creates problems, however. For example, a disease in one colony can quickly spread to
thousands of other colonies. And when the colonies are transported to another part of the country, they take the disease with
them. If a single diseased colony enters the United States, that
colony puts all the nation's bees at risk. In the past, when farms
were pollinated by local bees of varying species, it was much
harder for a disease to spread.

The destruction of habitats for wild bees also increases the
risk to agriculture. When many different species help with pollination, a disease to any one species poses less of a threat. Of the
many American crops that depend on insect pollination, more
than 80 percent rely on the honeybees alone. "We've gotten so
dependent on honeybees that if anything goes wrong with them,
we're stuck," warns Suzanne Batra of the U.S. Department of
Agriculture.

Alternatives to the Honeybee

One response to the dangers of depending solely on honeybees
has been to encourage the use of other species for pollination.
Leafcutter bees have been found to be very successful in pollinating alfalfa fields. When leafcutter bees were introduced in the
1960s, they increased seed production from one hundred pounds
per acre to more than a thousand pounds. The blue orchard bee
is also being studied as a pollinator. This solitary bee builds nests
in holes in wood. Researchers drilled holes in wooden blocks until
they discovered just the hole size that orchard bees like. It took
fourteen years to figure out how to house and move the bees,

but tests are promising. One blue orchard bee can pollinate as many fruit trees as thirty honeybees. And, because they can tolerate cooler weather than honeybees, blue orchard bees pollinate earlier in the year, which produces better fruit. Gardeners can buy starter kits to raise blue orchard bees in their yards—but remember, they don't produce any honey.

Another bee, the hornfaced bee, has been used for pollination in Japan since the 1930s and is now being introduced into the United States. And the humble bumblebee has been used to pollinate tomatoes in greenhouses since the 1980s. Before then, people had to shake the pollen from plant to plant themselves.

Habitat Destruction

The best way to help both bees and farmers is to protect the wild places where many different species of bees can live. But the problem of habitat destruction is getting worse. Less and less farmland is left uncultivated, and the chemical pesticides used in farming kill bees as well as the insect pests for which they are intended. Even before the mite crisis, many American bees were dying from insecticides. A particular problem is caused by pesticides in tiny micro-capsules, which are used to release the poison gradually. Some capsules are the size of pollen grains, and bees mistakenly bring them back to the hive, where the poison kills the entire colony.

There is hope for honeybees, however. Unlike some threatened species, bees have many devoted friends in the human world. Hundreds of thousands of Americans keep bees as a hobby, and many of them join bee societies to share information on important topics such as the latest treatments for bee diseases. And because billions of dollars worth of fruits, nuts, and vegetable

WILDFLOWERS RELY ON BEES FOR POLLINATION, AS DO AGRICULTURAL CROPS.

BEES AND HEALING

More than 40 million Americans—one out of every six people—suffer from arthritis, which causes pain, stiffness, and swelling in the hands, knees, and other joints. For more than two thousand years, people have claimed that bee stings ease the pain of people suffering from arthritis and other diseases. In many parts of the world, bee venom is used as a natural folk remedy for pain. Today, more and more people are turning to bee venom to treat chronic pain.

Using bee products as medicine is called apitherapy. George Mraz, a beekeeper in Middlebury, Vermont, suffered from painful arthritis in his knees. He had heard about bee venom therapy and considered it an old wives' tale, but the pain bothered him so much that he decided to give it a try. The very next day, he wrote in his 1995 book, *Health and the Honeybee*, "There wasn't a trace of pain or stiffness in my knees." Mraz suggested bee sting therapy to a neighbor, whose arthritis hurt his hands so much that he could barely milk his cows. Within a few weeks, he could move his hands again. Mraz helped start the American Apitherapy Society, which promotes bee venom therapy. Scientific studies are now being done to test the value of the chemicals in bee venom as medicine.

Bee venom therapy is simple: A bee is plucked from a jar with a pair of tweezers and held against the patient's skin until it stings. Each treatment may involve several stings. When performed safely, apitherapy may reduce pain and inflammation from disabling medical problems, making the treatment well worth a few dozen stings. But before people try it, they should be tested for allergies because bee stings can kill. A person allergic to bee stings can collapse, unable to breath, after one sting. Fortunately, 95 percent of people sensitive to bee stings are not allergic to honeybees, only to other species of bees or wasps.

Other bee products are used as medicine as well. Fresh honey is often put on wounds to heal them because it contains hydrogen peroxide and other chemicals that kill germs. And real apitherapy fans make it a point to eat not only lots of nutrient-rich, unfiltered honey but also royal jelly, the miracle food that makes larvae grow into adult bees and queens.

crops depend on bees, the agricultural industry has a stake in their future as well. Even in cities, many people raise "bee gardens" to provide flowers for bees. Anyone interested in learning more about these amazing creatures need only contact their local library or beekeeping club.

Glossary

abdomen—the rear section of an insect that contains the stomach

allergy—a negative reaction of the body to a protein

antenna—one of a pair of long, thin, flexible sensory organs attached to the head

caste—a group within a species that has a specialized form and set of tasks

cocoon—the covering that an insect larva makes for itself before changing to a pupa

colony—a large number of insects living together as a group

comb—a flat sheet of six-sided wax cells attached together in which bees store honey and raise their young; honeycomb

crop—a pouch inside an animal where food is stored after being swallowed, but not digested, and is later regurgitated, such as a bee's honey stomach

drone—a male bee

fertilize—combine male sperm and female egg in order to produce a new organism

forager—one who searches for food

gene—a section of DNA, a complex molecule containing a code for passing inherited traits from parents to children

habitat—place or environment where a plant or animal can live

hibernate—to pass the winter in a deep rest similar to sleep

hive—a colony of bees, or the container a colony lives in

larva—the early life stage of an insect after it comes out of the egg, when it resembles a wingless worm or grub

lens—the part of the eye through which light enters and is focused onto the retina

nectar—a sweet liquid produced by plants which bees collect and turn into honey

mead—an alcoholic drink made from fermented honey and water

metamorphosis—radical changes in shape and structure that a young insect makes as it develops into its adult form

pheromone—a chemical signal produced by an animal that stimulates a response from other animals of the same species

pollen—small particles of colored dust that are produced by male parts of flowers and must be carried to the female part of a flower for a seed to form

pollination—moving pollen from the male part of a flower to the female

proboscis—a tube connected to the head for sucking in food

propolis—a brownish, waxy substance gathered by bees from the buds of trees and used as glue

pupa—the middle stage of metamorphosis, in which a young insect changes from a larva to an adult, usually inside a cocoon

reproduction—creation of young from adults of the same species, who pass on their genes to their offspring

resin—an oily liquid produced by plants

social—living in large, organized groups

solitary—living completely alone

species—a particular kind of animal, whose members are all similar and can breed with one another

swarm—to leave the hive as a group, with a queen, in search of a location to start a new colony

thorax—the middle or chest section of an insect to which the wings and legs are attached

venom—poison created by an animal's body and injected into another animal by stinging or biting

Species Checklist

Bees have both common and scientific names. Common names can be confusing because some refer to an entire group of related species; others refer to a single species; and still others refer to certain bees within a species. Scientific names, in contrast, follow precise rules. Related species are grouped into a genus, and related genera are grouped in families. Individual species can also be divided into subspecies or races. There may also be small groups of genera within a family called tribes.

Scientific names for species consist of two Latin words: The first is the genus, and the second is the species. If the species is divided into races, a third name may be added at the end. All are italicized, but only the genus is capitalized. Family names are capitalized but not italicized. Common names are not italicized and are lowercased, unless they are taken from a proper noun.

Listed below are the common and scientific names for all the bees mentioned in this book. Keep in mind that this is far from a comprehensive list of all bee species. There are roughly 20,000 species in all.

Bee Families
cellophane bees (Colletidae family)
digger bees (Anthophoridae family)
honeybees and relatives (Apidae family)
leafcutter bees and mason bees (Megachilidae family)
mining bees (Andrenidae family)
sweat bees (Halictidae family)

Tribes in the Apidae Family
bumblebees (Bombini)
honeybees (Apini)
orchid bees (Euglossini)
stingless bees (Meliponinae)

Species of True Honeybees, in genus *Apis*, Family Apidae
common honeybees (*Apis mellifera*)
giant honeybees (*Apis dorsata* and *Apis laboriosa*)
dwarf honeybees (*Apis florea*)
Indian honeybees (*Apis cerana*)

Races of Apis mellifera
Cape bees (*Apis mellifera capensis*)
Carniolan bees (*Apis mellifera carnica*)
Caucasian bees (*Apis mellifera caucasica*)
East African bees (*Apis mellifera scutellata*)
Egyptian bees (*Apis mellifera lamarckii*)
German dark bees (*Apis mellifera mellifera*)
Italian honeybees (*Apis mellifera lingustica*)
Mountain bees (*Apis mellifera monticola*)
North African Tellian bees (*Apis mellifera intermissa*)
West African bees (*Apis mellifera adonsonii*)

Africanized honeybees or "killer bees" are the product of interbreeding between *Apis mellifera adonsonii* or *scutellata* and other *Apis mellifera* honeybees

Solitary Species
alfalfa leafcutter bees (*Megachile rotundata*)
alkali bees (*Nomia melanderi*)
blue orchard bees (*Osmia lignaria*)
hornfaced bees (*Osmia cornifrons*)

Hierarchy of Groups

Order Hymenoptera
▼
Suborder Apocrita
▼
Infraorder Aculeata
▼
Superfamily Apoidea
▼
Apiformes [bees]
▼
Family Apidae
▼
Subfamily Apinae
▼
Tribe Apini [honeybees]
▼
Apis mellifera [common honeybee]

Further Research

Books for Young People

Bonney, Richard E. *Beekeeping: A Practical Guide*. North Adams, MA: Storey, 1993.

Gleanings Staff. *The New Starting Right with Bees: A Beginner's Handbook on Beekeeping*. Medina, OH: Root, 1997.

Kerby, Mona. *Friendly Bees, Ferocious Bees*. New York: Franklin Watts, 1987.

Lavies, Bianca. *Killer Bees*. New York: E. P. Dutton, 1994.

Pringle, Laurence. *Killer Bees*. rev. ed. New York: Morrow Junior Books, 1990.

Web Sites

http://www.pbs.org/wgbh/nova/bees
A web site created by the PBS television program *NOVA*.

www.apitherapy.org
Information about the medicinal use of bees and bee products.

www.honey.com
A web site about honey with fun facts, games, and trivia.

http://bee.airoot.com/beeculture/index.htm
The web site for *Bee Culture*, a magazine for beekeepers.

http://ep.k12.ri.us/riverside/bee.html
A list of web sites on bees for middle school students.

Videos

Bees and How They Live, Chatsworth, CA: AIMS Multimedia, 1993

David Attenborough's The Private Life of Plants, vol. 3: The Birds and the Bees, Atlanta, GA: Turner Home Entertainment, 1995

The Swarm—India's Killer Bees, Burbank, CA: National Geographic Video, 2000

"Tales from the Hive" (NOVA), South Burlington, VT: WGBH-Boston Video, 2000

Bibliography

So many terrific writers have written wonderful books about bees that the books mentioned here barely scratch the surface. These are the ones I relied on the most in my own research:

Bailey, L., and B.V. Ball. *Honey Bee Pathology*, 2nd ed. San Diego: Academic Press, 1991. An overview of the many illnesses that afflict honeybees. Treatment methods are also discussed.

Crompton, John. *A Hive of Bees*. New York: The Lyons Press, 1987. A witty, engaging book by a talented author and former beekeeper who clearly enjoys and admires bees and their quirks.

Free, John B. *Bees and Mankind*. London: Unwin Hyman, 1982. A good introduction to solitary bees and bumblebees, as well as honeybees, with a fascinating review of the history of honey-hunting and bee-keeping around the world.

Gould, James L., and Carol Grant Gould. *The Honey Bee*. New York: W.H. Freeman, Co., 1995. A brilliant introduction to honeybees filled with superb color photos and written by active bee researchers who describe some astounding results.

More, Daphne. *The Bee Book: The History and Natural History of the Honeybee*. New York: David & Charles, 1976. A fascinating introduction to bees and beekeeping, with especially strong sections on the historical use of bee products and the development of beekeeping in Europe.

Morse, Roger A. *Bee and Beekeeping*. Ithaca: Cornell University Press, 1975. A thorough, clear, and informative discussion of honeybees and bee-keeping by a professor at Cornell University.

Winston, Mark L. *The Biology of the Honey Bee*. Cambridge, MA: Harvard University Press, 1991. A concise yet authoritative review of the vast scientific research on honeybees. Includes descriptions of body parts and glands, chemical communication, and honeybee subspecies.

Index

Page numbers for illustrations are in **boldface**.

About the Author

MARTIN SCHWABACHER has written several books for children on science topics. He also writes for the American Museum of Natural History's exhibitions, courses, and web sites. He grew up in Minnesota and currently lives in New York City with children's writer Melissa McDaniel (whose first name means "honeybee") and their daughter, Iris.